MAKING
COMPUTERS PAY

MAKING COMPUTERS PAY

JOHN GRAHAM

A HALSTED PRESS BOOK

JOHN WILEY & SON
New York

Published in the U.S.A.
by Halsted Press, a Division
of John Wiley & Sons, Inc.
New York
Printed in Great Britain

ISBN 0470-32086-9

Library of Congress Catalog Card 75-17430

Printed in Great Britain

in 10 point Times Roman type

Preface

There are many people in industry today who have been given cause to harbour doubts about the value of computers and have perhaps regretted becoming involved with computer projects. Individual careers have sometimes been affected by having too much, or too little, faith in computer projects. Some companies have been through lean periods which they attribute to the failure of their computerisation plans. However, for all the failures that may have occurred there are also success stories, and the purpose of this book is to help managers to appreciate factors which contribute to success.

The thesis of this book is to show how data-processing costs can be estimated and controlled and to give guidance to management in ensuring that projects which are implemented are relevant to the needs of the organisation. Some of the issues affecting these key objectives are concerned with large questions like the development of organisational policy, but the treatment of these issues is straightforward, and, I hope, free of unnecessary jargon.

It is odd that the most senior people in organisations should find computer projects so troublesome, but it is often the case. Men who have the foresight and energy to create successful and complex business operations become bemused by the intricacies of computerisation and the impact that it has on their organisation. We cannot expect that the most senior people in companies will have time to learn all about hardware and software, and to keep up with the massive output of technical information that the computer industry generates. The answer must be to leave that task to the computer professionals. The problem is, of course, that computer people are human and prone to make errors; what is more, computer people are not usually good businessmen. The heart of the matter is to know how to monitor the computer function, to know what you can expect from the machine and from computer people, and to develop a realisation of the penalties of not exerting a proper control over computer projects and computer people.

Computers may be complex, but the rules for evaluating projects and monitoring their successful execution are no more complex or arduous than those required to manage other aspects of business. Failures in harnessing the potential of computers occur in large technically based organisations, like airlines and oil companies, as well as among the first-time users of computers. The reason for this is not difficult to find. The computer is not usually the mainstream activity of the business; at least, it

7

75611

does not always appear to be. The people who reach general management level within a company are not specialists in computing, even if they have received some training in the subject. The data processing function is a support service to management, and many managers feel that it is less important than the production or marketing functions of the business.

Computers do absorb money – the sole reason for their existence is that they are an investment in achieving greater efficiency and enhancing the service that the organisation can provide. The sums of money involved are, however, considerable, and significant returns require a great deal of dedicated effort. Almost every computer project has some element of the unknown about it, and rigorous control is required to ensure that problems can be anticipated before they can jeopardise the return expected.

I have shown in Chapter 1, Figure 1.2 (page 19), a typical budget for a data processing department. The money involved is significant: it is expected that an established company of reasonable size will spend between 1 per cent and 2 per cent of its turnover on data processing.

In recent years, the cost of hardware has tended to reduce in relation to the cost of the people involved in data processing, and the efficient use of people is particularly significant in curtailing unnecessary expenditure in data processing. An important part of the management process is to motivate the computer staff to understand the significance of their contribution to the organisation.

Computer staff are generally expensive in relation to other people employed in the business. They are also creative people who can get a sense of satisfaction out of their work, but it is true as well that their work can provide this satisfaction in a very abstract sense. They have a complete language of their own, designed, it seems, to confuse other people, and full of powerful concepts which may have no immediate relevance to the business. The essence of managing the data processing function is to harness the creativity of these people in ways which will make a direct contribution to the organisation.

An operations director of an independent airline once said to me, 'I run a very complex technical business – we fly a fleet of advanced aircraft around the globe. We use computers to help us and to enable us to grow efficiently. But I do not want a reputation for developing the most advanced computer systems. Our reputation is made by flying aircraft efficiently and on schedule.' At the time he was considering a systems proposal which had many intangible benefits, and he sensibly set the proposal aside for two years and the company continued to operate to its normal high standard, successfully challenging bigger organisations which had a massive investment in data processing. I believe that this hard-nosed attitude was right and underlines one of the fundamental tasks of top management. They must establish priorities in data processing and involve themselves in the evaluation of data processing projects and the contribution of the projects to their business.

Too often one observes data processing departments which have established a momentum of their own, introducing techniques which are of little benefit to their company.

Computers are intended to be of service to managers. The costs of any proposed computer project should be significantly covered by the benefits which it brings. It should be the responsibility of line management to bring these benefits into the company, with the aid of data processing people. It is the responsibility of data processing people to evaluate the nature and costs of systems needed and to develop and operate the systems successfully.

In the development of systems, data processing people are particularly dependent upon the line departments that they serve. In any new system, there are many features which have to be introduced requiring changes of attitude and method on the part of line personnel. The management of line departments have also to be involved in making timely decisions about the nature and scope of projects. If there is little understanding between data processing people and management, extensive delays can occur in the design and implementation of systems. These delays are extremely expenpensive, not only in wasting the time and energy of data processing people and line personnel, but also in delaying the benefits that the system introduces.

The various chapters of this book are arranged to identify principles to be adopted by management in dealing with computer people and computer projects. At the end of each chapter there is a check list which summarises the main points given in the chapter and provides a ready guide to the attitudes and policies which will help managers get the most out of their computer departments. Of course, the book does not deal with all the many technical problems that computer people encounter, and neither does it identify all the mistakes which computer people can commit. Perhaps, by concentrating on the general problems of controlling and monitoring computer projects, I have emphasised too much the responsibility of line management. For that I offer no apology. This is not a book for technicians; it deals with simple management concepts that are too often overlooked in the hustle of our business life. I am sure that computer people will also benefit from the study of these principles, since those of us who have developed our careers in data processing need continually to remind ourselves of the support that we owe to general and line management. The computer department is intended as a servant of management and not its master.

I have opened this book in Chapter 1 with a discussion of the organisational problems relating to computers and the management of companies. The examples in this first chapter are drawn from large organisations, but the principles apply in smaller ones. If the computer is to serve management, how can we best ensure that management is able to control computer people, and, at the same time, enable the computer and systems specialists adequately to look after their own responsibility of creating systems which service the whole organisation without undue duplication

9

of costs? What are the benefits and penalties of centralised control over data processing, and how does this relate to the autonomy of line managers?

Chapter 2 continues this theme by stressing the obligations and commitments that line managers have to data processing projects, while the organisation and reporting structures which lead to successful project implementation are described. The key stages of projects are identified and the responsibility for monitoring and controlling the project is explained.

Chapter 3 examines the elements of project control at a much more detailed level, and discusses the problems associated with setting up a project and maintaining impetus through to completion. It deals with the change of management emphasis throughout the project, and the annex to the chapter includes a system of documentation to provide the right environment for project control and management. This documentation is reproduced by the kind permission of Dataskil, a subsidiary company of International Computers Limited.

The selection and justification of data processing projects is one of the most important tasks facing senior management of organisations. In Chapter 4, we lay stress on the need for a formal approach to project selection and suggest a simple method of cost-benefit analysis together with a check list of questions which will enable management to examine critically the merits of projects presented for consideration.

In Chapter 5, I have dealt with another area in which the senior management of organisations can greatly influence the success of a company's systems. A straightforward policy for controlling the funding of data processing projects is explained, and the dangers inherent in leaving this issue to be resolved on an ad hoc basis are examined.

In Chapter 6, I have taken a critical look at the concept of the total management information system. The complete integration of an organisation's procedures into a totally cohesive system is not an impossible or unreasonable objective, but it is one which will place a great strain on both line management and the data processing department. It could be that the effort does not bring worthwhile benefits into the organisation and a simpler approach might prove to be more effective in improving the company's performance. It is a responsibility of top management to decide on this issue, and Chapter 6 provides the arguments to help them analyse their own situation.

The terms *MIS* and *database* go together, and many of the arguments for and against *MIS* systems apply equally well to data management systems.

In Chapter 7, I have asked the question ,'Do you need database management?' The objective in this chapter is once more to provide questions and answers which will be helpful to managers in considering the answers to their own database requirements. The benefits of data management systems are explained, and some of the penalties are identified.

Chapter 8 explores many issues concerned with buying software and analyses the attitudes and motives of the buyer and vendor. It is in this area that companies make decisions which will have a lasting effect upon their organisation. The chapter helps managers to understand the risks which they are taking when buying software services and describes safeguards which should be taken in negotiations.

Chapter 9 is a survey of the systems audit field and provides guidelines for setting up an audit of the systems and data processing functions.

In the final chapter, I have looked at the area of computer operations, and have attempted to show how much inefficiency there can be which passes undetected. The modern general purpose computer is rarely fully utilised, and there are always methods for improving throughput and productivity in almost any computer room. However, the issues involved are complex and have a great deal of interaction. This aspect of data processing is one in which the management of organisations may well have to rely upon expert advice, but Chapter 10 will provide a grasp of the issues involved while identifying areas where investigation is likely to be worthwhile.

Computers are here to stay, and they are being made to pay their way. There is no need for any manager to be confused by the complexity of the computer itself. The principles involved in managing computer projects are simple enough. The important issue is not to be overawed by the technology, but to strengthen the will to manage the computer. We can establish targets for the data processing function, just as we can for any other discipline; we can measure achievement in meeting those targets and take corrective action when results do not meet the required standards considered to be necessary for the efficiency of the organisation. If management does this successfully, it can compel the computer people to think in positive terms about their contribution to the organisation that they serve.

I hope that my book will impart confidence to management and encourage them to invest their time in fruitful involvement with computer projects.

Woking

JOHN GRAHAM

Contents

Figures

Chapter 1

Setting a Basis for the Control of Cost Effectiveness

Effective control of the costs and benefits of computerisation is a responsibility at many levels in the organisation. It is clear that individual projects must be properly evaluated and controlled, but the whole basis for control at this level can be undermined if the right organisational policies are not established. This first chapter is therefore devoted to a discussion of these overriding issues.

Some of the examples used in the chapter are drawn from large organisations, but the principles apply in organisations using computers for the first time. In any case, whatever the size of the organisation, the issues are worthy of consideration, because effective policies have to be generated before the organisation is allowed to develop characteristics which will militate against ultimate success in computerisation.

The data processing function is a support service to the management of an organisation. Sometimes the whole philosophy of a business may be such that its products and services have no viability without the use of computing power, but we cannot escape the conclusion that the data processing department's purpose is to support either the manufacturing, marketing, distribution or administration within the organisation. The computer should be a servant to management and not an end in itself.

This conclusion seems to imply that the data processing department should be prepared to operate at the behest of the operating divisions of the organisation, responding to every request or demand for its services. It is possible for a data processing unit to sustain a very successful image by so doing, but it is not the best approach for the efficiency of the company within which it operates. I will develop my reasons for this assertion a little later on, but first let us consider some of the ways in which data processing can develop if no particular policies are established.

In the first instance, computer units will be set up wherever there is a recognisable information-handling problem. It is likely that parts of an organisation situated in the same geographical locality will collaborate over and at least use a single installation. However, there are many precedents to show that this obvious step is not always taken. Computers tend to arise in units which have large enough budgets to afford the initial investment, and every year thereafter the operating costs increase as the work of the installation expands to meet the exploding demands of managers for more information.

Figure 1.1 *Staff required for a medium-sized data processing department.*

Job title	Numbers
Data processing manager	1
Operations manager	1
Systems and programming manager	1
Secretarial and administration	3
Systems analysts	3
Programmers	8
Shift leaders	3
Senior operators	3
Operators	3
Data control clerks	4
Punch operators	4
TOTAL:	34

Assumptions:
(a) Capital cost of computer configuration: £250K.
(b) Operators working on a three-shift basis.

(See Figure 1.2 for breakdown of budget)

In undertakings which are organised into autonomous divisions (say, by virtue of distinctive products, or for geographical or functional differences) it is not unusual to find that each division has its own data processing department. In practice, this often means that different computer ranges are used and therefore that there are tremendous constraints upon the possibility of spreading the costs, or sharing the benefits, of the applications developed. This attitude is prevalent in government agencies, as well as in industrial organisations. For example, in the United Kingdom at the time of writing, very little hardware standardisation has taken place in the gas and electricity supply industries, or in the medical field.

I do not wish to argue here in favour of hardware standardisation for its own sake, for there are some important arguments against commitment to a particular range of equipment:

(a) No organisation likes to put itself in the hands of a single supplier.
(b) Hardware suitable for one area of application may not be suitable for another.
(c) Commercial considerations may favour selection of different suppliers at different times.

18

(d) The availability of software for use with particular hardware systems may also influence the situation.

Figure 1.2 *Annual budget for a medium-sized data processing department.*

Budget heading	Department		
	Operations	Systems Programming	Total
	£K	£K	£K
Labour			
Salaries	42·0	40·0	82·0
Overtime	4·0	2·0	6·0
Social security	2·0	2·0	4·0
Pensions	2·0	2·0	4·0
Indirect labour			
Training	1·2	1·0	2·2
Expenses	0·5	1·0	1·5
Welfare	1·5	1·5	3·0
Accommodation			
Rent and rates	35·0	14·0	49·0
Power	7·5	0·5	8·0
Cleaning	2·0	0·5	2·5
Laundry	0·2	—	0·2
Security	5·0	—	5·0
Transport	1·0	—	1·0
Telephones	3·0	—	3·0
Equipment			
Machine rental	50·0	—	50·0
Maintenance	15·0	—	15·0
Consumables			
Paper and stationery	5·5	1·0	6·5
Cards and ribbons	1·0	—	1·0
Replacement media	1·5	—	1·5
£K	179·9	65·5	245·4

There is also a strong advocacy to recognise that one should not interfere with the decisions of autonomous divisional units which are performing well, e.g. in terms of the profit they make, or their cost effectiveness in providing service to the public. I have met many individual directors who will argue that the only thing which they need to supply to their holding companies is a specified level of return on capital and a few sheets of figures periodically to show the general performance and condition of their division. 'What I do with my data processing is my affair', they argue, and one has a degree of sympathy with their view.

In a company which has a genuinely divisionalised structure, it may be sensible for data processing policies to be developed at divisional level. If a company has pursued this policy, then perhaps it will have avoided many of the unedifying arguments which surround the ownership of computing power. It is to be hoped, however, that each of the divisions will have pursued and operated consistent policies for themselves.

One must also be careful not to be deluded into thinking that a company is divisionalised when, in reality, the so-called divisions are merely manufacturing in different localities, or servicing the same product but in different ways. If different divisions are dealing with the same basic information and applications, they should not be treated as independent in data processing matters.

Let us leave this discussion for now and consider some of the areas in which there is a need to establish policies, and discuss the reasons which justify the importance of such policies.

Minimising Costs by Centralising Services
The costs of a data processing department are not confined to the hardware alone; for the purpose of discussion, Figure 1.3 depicts some figures

Figure 1.3 *Approximate breakdown of expenditure in a large data processing department.*

1	Hardware	35%
2	Computer operations staff	22%
3	Systems and programming staff	30%
4	Other*	13%
		100%

*Includes training, external services, supplies.

which we can consider to be a typical breakdown of costs for a large computer installation, i.e. one in which expenditure budgets are, say, around £500,000. The hardware is, of course, very significant, and represents a very tangible cost item upon which to exert control. It is difficult to say, outside a specific case, that centralised control of hardware is more effective, but there are some superficial arguments in favour of having the greater part of the computing power in one physical location rather than spread over a number of independent sites.

(a) Each independent computer will require an initial investment in environmental conditioning, say £40K for a medium-sized machine.
(b) Many applications in remote places can be driven via terminals.
(c) The staff costs in operating the equipment should be considerably reduced by operating a larger central configuration, as against two or more independent sites.
(d) Scheduling, loading and utilisation of equipment and storage media

are more effectively controlled, thus leading to more rational control over the purchase of additional equipment.

Providing Effective Service
These arguments indicate that the first two items listed in Figure 1.3 can be more effectively controlled by operating computers as a central bureau on behalf of the various using departments. The main advantages of this approach are:

(a) Principal areas of cost are more readily controlled.
(b) There are better opportunities for staff development within the data processing function.
(c) Costs to independent using departments should be minimised.
(d) Consistent operational standards can be developed.

The effectiveness of this approach will, in practice, rely heavily upon the management team set up to manage a bureau; it must run as a very professional unit able to provide an efficient, accurate and timely service to its users. It should recover its costs from using departments without charging exorbitant rates. Above all, each user's problem should be looked at with complete objectivity, and when the need for a local dedicated hardware system presents itself, the case should be recognised and dealt with accordingly. A slightly less complicated decision may then need to be taken: should the local hardware system be locally owned and controlled, or be run by the central bureau?

I propose to leave this question until the end of the chapter, when we will have considered policies relating to application development.

The Need for Application Policies
The most persistent reasons for dissatisfaction with computers are concerned not with the reliability of the hardware itself, but with the inability to get applications working effectively, on time, and within levels of expenditure originally forecast. The accuracy of the results provided by the system may also be in question, and what is perhaps more disturbing to top management is that information emanating from different systems run by different departments is frequently contradictory or incompatible.

I do not wish to discuss all of these symptoms in this chapter, but would like to discuss the problems relating to the quality and reliability of information.

There are, I suppose, two extreme situations which management can foster:

(a) Independent systems dedicated to particular applications, with no regard to the relationship with other systems within the organisation.
(b) Highly integrated systems in which applications share common files of data and are thus able to generate compatible management information.

21

There is, of course, a middle way in which both types of system can be developed according to the need of the organisation. The difficulty for the management services manager is to find this solution. It takes a very brave and well-informed individual to do this on his own; it is one of those areas in which data processing policy is essential, and very few boards of directors really find time to understand the issues involved. They do, however, get very irritated and frustrated by the conditions which arise in the absence of such policies.

Figure 1.4 isolates some of the factors for and against integrated systems, and systems dedicated to particular applications.

Figure 1.4   *Arguments for and against integrated systems.*

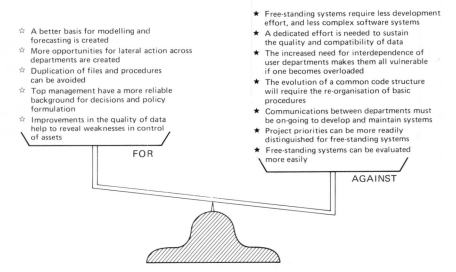

☆ A better basis for modelling and forecasting is created

☆ More opportunities for lateral action across departments are created

☆ Duplication of files and procedures can be avoided

☆ Top management have a more reliable background for decisions and policy formulation

☆ Improvements in the quality of data help to reveal weaknesses in control of assets

FOR

★ Free-standing systems require less development effort, and less complex software systems

★ A dedicated effort is needed to sustain the quality and compatibility of data

★ The increased need for interdependence of user departments makes them all vulnerable if one becomes overloaded

★ The evolution of a common code structure will require the re-organisation of basic procedures

★ Communications between departments must be on-going to develop and maintain systems

★ Project priorities can be more readily distinguished for free-standing systems

★ Free-standing systems can be evaluated more easily

AGAINST

The main problem with integrated systems is that they take longer to develop. This is not usually on account of technical problems, but stems from the fact that more people need to be involved in both setting the initial objectives and designing and implementing the procedures. The more people involved, the greater the communication problem – and the longer the duration of the project.

There have always been some technical difficulties with the implementation of integrated management information systems, but improvements in general purpose software available for this purpose have progressively minimised this problem. We will look at this topic more closely in Chapter 8, but at this stage merely say that flexible software enables data processers to develop applications which can be adapted to reflect changing company requirements and enable different applications to use the same database. These are essential characteristics of a management information system.

The importance, or otherwise, of a well-developed management information system can only be assessed in the context of a particular organisation at any moment in time. It will probably be inappropriate to delay the development of key applications in order to integrate them with other company procedures if there are substantial benefits from early implementation of the key applications.

However, this does not mean that the eventual objective of a common management information should be pursued. The factors which contribute to the construction of an orderly management information system can be taken into account, and include:

(a) The design of standard coding systems to represent information in both internal computer procedures and external documentation.
(b) The use of flexible software systems which will permit flexibility in the subsequent adaptation of systems.
(c) The development of interface specifications which recognise the requirements to pass information between different applications.

These are relatively feasible technical requirements which data processers should be capable of organising. However, they do not materialise spontaneously where different divisions or user departments are allowed to dictate the objectives and timescales of particular projects without consideration. They will certainly not arise in organisations which have allowed different departments and divisions to run their own systems and programming departments, and it is one of the factors to be considered in assessing the level of centralisation or decentralisation over data-processing activity. To develop integrated information systems, centralised direction of system development is essential.

Symptoms of Weakness in the Direction of Applications
The reader may well consider that I have over-emphasised the need for some central direction over applications, but I list below some of the symptoms that I have observed in companies which have not established effective applications policies:

(a) In a company manufacturing capital equipment, the sales director, the production director and the chief accountant reported very different figures for the order-taking rate and the level of outstanding orders.
(b) A department responsible for producing corporate plans and budgets operated on incorrect and irreconcilable data about current and previous events within the company.
(c) A finance director had very little information to assess the health and prospects of various subsidiary companies around the world, and could not make accurate global forecasts.
(d) A company manufacturing similar products in four localities had

23

developed four different production control systems and could not ensure that identical components used in different products were commonly identified.

One will find similar situations in almost any company or enterprise that is examined, and the reason for having some central direction over applications will usually be to:

(a) Avoid costly duplication in the design of systems and software.
(b) Provide more reliable and consistent management information, to enable the activities of different units to be more effectively co-ordinated.
(c) Allow the development of the total organisation to be made in a more objective and informed atmosphere.

I believe it is for this reason that many companies which have highly decentralised their operations will continue to attempt some centralised control over their data processing.

The problem, however, is to do this in such a way as not to stifle local initiatives and inspirations. Operating divisions must be able to achieve their objectives without being encumbered by systems which do not respond to their requirements. Let us consider next the view of a division which requires autonomy in the direction of its management services function.

Arguments for Local Control over Data Processing

In order to simplify control in a multi-divisional organisation, the central management will often encourage, and stress, the concept of local autonomy. This is a good way to develop managers – making them responsible at an early age and improving their motivation and performance. There is particular emphasis on this form of control in international companies where there may be political and cultural reasons for giving control to local nationals. Once this atmosphere is created among divisions, it extends naturally to all functional units within a local organisation, e.g. it applies equally to the management accountant and the data processing manager of any particular division. The local functional manager is thus subject to two conflicting pressures:

(a) To support and satisfy the local management.
(b) To operate within standards and policies established by the corporate functional manager.

Now the conditions within a subsidiary or autonomous division may be radically different from those prevailing in the parent company. It is natural to conclude that the local functional manager will identify more readily with the problems and people in his local organisation, and will only operate within any corporate policies that may exist if they are:

(a) Not unduly restrictive in discharging local responsibilities.
(b) Are seen by him to have genuine benefits to the corporation.
(c) Are enforced by a recognised central authority.

In multi-divisional companies, poor comunication between the corporate data processing function and the local data processing managers will easily lead to a breakdown in understanding. It goes without saying that poor communications between the director of any local division and the corporate management will also severely restrict the development or implementation of practical policies for the data processing function. Such attitudes can stem from a resentment of control from the centre, or from fear that undue burdens are being placed upon the local enterprise.

Typical reactions from local managers include:

'We already have effective local systems. Why should we change?'
'Your systems present too heavy an overhead for us.'
'You do not understand our business.'
'Your systems do not take account of our local requirements.'
'We wish to concentrate on a particular problem.'
'We do not wish to lose control over any aspect of our business, we haven't confidence in involving ourselves with other people's problems.'
'We use different hardware and software from you.'
'We use different standards.'
'We need simple systems – our organisation is not ready for a complex implementation programme.'
'We haven't any money to spend.'
'We haven't got enough staff of suitable quality.'

Some of these objections are of relatively minor significance, and can be overcome by discussion and management action. Those which have their roots in personal and inter-divisional relationships may be less easy to solve.

Identifying the Corporate Policies

Having stated some conflicting issues which affect computing policies in multidivisional companies, let us now formulate practical solutions.

In the first place, it is necessary to see that the reasons for having any form of central influence are understood, and that individual policies established to exert such influence are conducive to:

(a) Improving corporate control and co-ordination.
(b) Reducing the duplication of costs and achieving a better utilisation of resources.

25

The degree of corporate control desired is a key factor in assessing how far one should go in establishing corporate data processing policies. The nature, quality, structure and quantity of information needed play an important part in this evaluation. An analysis of the information required to flow between different divisions and between them and the central management is the first step in evolving a data processing policy.

An Information Policy

The simplest situation to co-ordinate is one in which the central body determines the reports, analyses and statistics that it wishes to receive from different divisions, and allows them to pursue independent data processing developments provided that the central requirement is fulfilled. Companies which adopt a policy of this sort will need some central unit to develop and maintain code books that provide standards under which information is reported to the centre. The reports themselves can be in the form of final printed results or in some machine readable form for processing at the centre. If these reports are solely of a financial nature, the central finance group will be responsible for the standards and their enforcement.

The central data processing unit may need to act in a consultancy capacity to assist those divisions which do not feel able to develop systems that can provide the information needed by the centre. In such cases, the central management have a case to question whether the local division has good enough systems adequately to control its operation. In practice, one often finds that the local system is good enough to provide local control, but not easily capable of extension to meet further requirements. Whatever the case, clearly this situation provides an opportunity for the corporate data processing unit to see that duplication is avoided and to encourage the local units to adopt systems developed centrally.

A more complex situation arises where different divisions are concerned with the same events and related information. The tendency is for the divisions to start by developing systems which meet their own internal requirements and to pass on information at convenient intervals to one another. This rarely works well without considerable duplication of effort, in both the development and day-to-day running of systems. What is probably far worse is that the different systems are irreconcilable and provide different answers to the same question. In a company where this situation exists, nothing will happen to improve things unless top management takes decisive action to encourage a single system to be developed across the functional units involved.

A system of this nature is an obvious candidate for development by the central data processing unit, although it, in turn, will need to involve line and data processing staff from the operating divisions.

There may also be systems where, as a matter of policy, the corporate management require each operating division, whether it has its own data processing unit or not, to use a standard company system. For example, many large industrial organisations insist upon a standard system for personnel administration, the purpose being, say, to ensure:

(a) That common records exist for staff within the group to provide for similar assessment and development programmes for individuals.
(b) That the potential mobility of staff across divisions is improved.
(c) That a corporate manpower planning programme can be operated.

Here again, the central data processing unit has to co-ordinate and develop the system, allowing for flexibility to meet particular local requirements; and, again, consultation and involvement with local data processing and line personnel is essential.

By first tracking the information flow and applications within an organisation, the relationship between divisional units becomes clearer. The following types of system are candidates for direct central control:

(a) Those which are required to operate across divisional boundaries.
(b) Those which, for policy reasons, are to be implemented within divisions in a standard manner.
(c) Those which operate primarily within corporate departments.

In addition the following systems are candidates for development under the guidance and influence of a central data processing unit:

(a) Systems which provide information to corporate departments.
(b) Systems which operate upon data supplied by corporate departments.

The systems which remain can be said to be within the direct control of the local divisions themselves, and the nature and extent of central control may be determined after considering the costs and potential duplication of resources which arise from having data processing resources in local divisions.

Towards a Policy for Systems Responsibility
Once having established a need for the development of local systems, there are a variety of ways of organising the relationships between central and local data processing functions. To allow the divisions to go entirely their own way is bound to cause trouble in the long run; but to deny the local divisions the number and quality of people required to develop their applications is highly foolish. The following should provide a basis for an organisational policy:

(a) The corporate data processing manager should be responsible for technical standards for system development and for monitoring their correct use.
(b) If the local units are to use a central computer installation for running

27

their applications, then the corporate department would be best suited to develop the computer procedures; but the local unit should develop the job requirement specification and approve the system design and implementation plans.

(c) If the local unit has problems which require dedicated hardware and a substantial ongoing commitment for systems and software expertise, then they should be allowed to develop their systems within the standards set by the corporate data processing manager.

(d) The corporate data processing manager should be given terms of reference and support to:

    (i) decide the responsibility for developing particular applications;
    (ii) monitor developments to encourage the exploitation of the systems and software produced;
    (iii) take an early interest in influencing any aspect of design which will improve or sustain corporate objectives.

A Hardware Policy

The hardware itself may be of secondary importance if the relationship between elements of the organisation requires very little exchange of information. In this case, divisions can be left to procure hardware on the terms best suited to their own local projects, but subject to policies existing for the acquisition and disposal of capital equipment within the organisation.

I personally would prefer always to institute a policy whereby the purchase or hire of data processing equipment has to be sanctioned by the corporate data processing manager as part of the capital approval procedure. He can comment particularly on the following issues:

(a) Whether the equipment breaches any important standardisation programme.
(b) Whether the application to be undertaken justifies the equipment.
(c) Whether the application can be tackled using existing installations, with or without enhancements.
(d) Whether adequate use has been obtained of any capital equipment to be replaced.

The standardisation upon hardware of a particular range is vital where the divisions concerned have common applications and problems. In this way important developments can be transferred from one division to another. The configurations can also be standardised to provide back-up in the event of hardware failure. This may imply setting rules for the design of the applications themselves; at least to the extent that the core storage and peripherals utilised must be within prescribed standards.

Where the corporate data processing manager is charged with the responsibility for ensuring that adequate use is made of data processing equipment, this responsibility needs to be strengthened by the authority to audit the efficiency of particular installations and to report the effective use of equipment.

These proposals are really instruments to put into effect the policies previously mentioned.

(a) To control the effective use of equipment and resources throughout the organisation.
(b) To protect any necessary standardisation programme.

They may be resented by the local data processing departments and line managers, and the practice of enforcing the policy must therefore be enlightened and helpful to the divisions concerned. All discussions impinging upon these issues should take place in an objective atmosphere.

A Software Policy
In the context of this section I define software as being:

Major programmes (supplied by computer manufacturers, or software houses, or developed internally) to perform general purpose functions helpful to a general class of computer user rather than for a particular application.

The smaller users of computers will rarely develop any major item of software, but users of medium and large size computers may often do so. There are three major interests to be looked after in controlling the use of software within any company having several installations:

(a) Internally developed software, or software commissioned from outside agencies, is expensive and the purpose may already be served by some existing item of software.
(b) The software may benefit several installations as well as the one originating the software.
(c) The use of a particular software item may impose standards which hinder the transfer of a system to other users.

If the local control of hardware has been granted to the divisional data processing units, it is important not to erode this by constraining them to use particular software methods in achieving their objectives. The control of software is probably best achieved through the same mechanism as is established to review applications; that is, provided no important standardisation policies are breached, local software should be permitted to develop.

Software developments are, however, very expensive, and there is therefore a case for keeping software budgets centrally to ensure that similar controls are imposed as for hardware acquisition. As in all areas effecting

29

centralisation/decentralisation, a helpful attitude by the central authority is necessary.

It may be that the creation of a central software bureau will provide the necessary expertise and professionalism to ensure that all divisions have adequate support while maintaining common standards. Any central service of this sort has to be available when people require it. If major implementation delays are experienced by a division through lack of central support, the policy is counter-productive and the causes will need to be eliminated.

I feel personally that to disallow local initiatives in exploiting and developing software bites too deeply into the preserve of any local systems manager. It will certainly not encourage him to be open about planned developments, and therefore, on balance, it will *not* lead to the ready transfer of technology from one centre to another.

A Policy for Systems Audit

This is a matter which invokes much argument, but one which can result in a policy which settles ultimately the responsibility for systems within a corporation. It is an important issue, and I have therefore decided to devote Chapter 9 to a fuller discussion. Let me say at this stage that where the tendency is to grant more autonomy to local divisions in developing systems, a strong central auditing function should be established to ensure that systems are effective in their operation and in the utilisation of resources.

In most companies, this authority will often rest with the internal audit department. I have formed the opinion that, in the hands of the right manager, the corporate data processing function can provide a powerful influence when given responsibility for systems audit throughout the corporation. The manager can help both to identify weaknesses and to use his resources to back up local divisions in overcoming them.

Personnel Policies

This policy must try to bridge the opposing desires of the corporate data processing manager and the local management.

The corporate data processing man may, at the extreme, wish to make all senior appointments in local data processing establishments, thus providing people who will be more disposed to understand and follow his policies while being, at the same time, satisfied that the local division is supported with data processing executives of the right calibre. On the other hand, the local directors may well wish to appoint a data processing manager of their own choice: one who suits their style of management, and because, and perhaps more significantly, the right to make this appointment is more in keeping with the prerogatives of an autonomous division.

It is likely that the local data processing executives will play a crucial role in the operation of the separate divisions and need to be clearly identi-

30

fied as members of the local management team. The main task of the data processing manager in a subsidiary company or division is to assist the management there in achieving its fundamental economic objectives. Therefore it is preferable that there should be a direct line responsibility to the local line management; and a dotted line responsibility to the corporate data processing manager for policy matters.

However, senior local appointments should be made at least with the advice and assistance of the corporate data processing manager, and, ideally, he should provide candidates to be interviewed for local positions. When an appointment is made, the executive concerned should be attached to the division to achieve specific objectives, and his future development may then be to another data processing appointment in the corporation, or perhaps into line management locally. If there is a well-established manpower development programme in the organisation, it should not be difficult to control this process and to provide opportunity for both local management and corporate data processing management to take part.

It makes sense for the corporate data processing manager to develop policies and facilities for the training and development of all data processing staff – his department will be well able to do this if its members have been successfully involved in establishing technical standards throughout the corporation. All this may not be practical in international corporations, where problems of distance and language intervene.

The objections of local management may not be simply reactions to corporate authority, but may come from general fear that data processing people do not understand the business problems existing in user departments. It is usually good practice to insist that project teams established to create major systems include good people from line departments who are trained in systems techniques and who may be asked to lead project teams. Conversely, data processing people should be seeded into line departments for periods.

If the corporate data processing manager can sustain, over a lengthy period, policies for this sort of cross-fertilisation, there should develop between data processing and user departments a greater mutual confidence making for more effective implementation.

SUMMARY OF CHAPTER 1

1   The management services and data processing functions should be situated organisationally, so that they can support the principal operating units of the organisation in achieving their objectives.

2   The point to which a manager of these support services reports should be such that he is able to participate with the general management in formulating and planning principal objectives.

3   The success of the management services function depends to a large degree upon the personality of the man chosen to lead the function and the

31

authority that he commands by virtue of his reputation, experience and objectivity.

4   The management services or data processing resources should not be totally subservient to the differing needs of line managers, but should be deployed to induce new concepts and methods that help the organisation as a whole in meeting its main objectives.

5   The top management of an organisation will need to formulate policies which create an environment in which computers can be successfully exploited.

6   If no appropriate policies are established, the data processing function will develop in a haphazard manner and will not achieve the desired benefits to the organisation without undue costs and organisational friction.

7   If top management does not get to grips with this problem sufficiently early, the result may be duplication of hardware resources and skilled manpower, together with systems which are incompatible.

8   Within the constraints imposed by priorities established by management, it is practical to plan systems such that they can be mutually coherent and aid co-ordination of the total activities of the group.

9   Compatible code structures, hardware standardisation and the development of flexible software systems can each aid the gradual integration of the organisation's information systems.

10   This aim is not always an ideal objective for an organisation in the short term, but generally proves to be desirable once immediate problems have been surmounted.

11   A coherent company system will not emerge spontaneously without the active participation of senior management.

12   Where this objective is sought, a substantial degree of centralised control over data processing is essential.

13   Local objections to centralised control should be recognised.

14   Central control should only be exerted where it can improve corporate co-ordination and control, or reduce the duplication of costs on a substantial scale.

15   The key to developing applications which improve corporate co-ordination is to analyse the information required at various management levels throughout the group.

16   In a multi-divisional organisation with independent data processing departments, the corporate data processing manager should be given terms of reference to influence the work of the various divisions to develop systems which encourage corporate co-ordination.

17   These terms of reference should include:
(a)   Approval of systems objectives.
(b)   Approval of code structures.
(c)   Control of hardware procurement and standardisation.
(d)   Responsibility for software standardisation.
(e)   Responsibility for auditing systems.

32

(f) Influence in the selection of key personnel for data processing appointments throughout the group.

18 Success in discharging these responsibilities will be achieved only if the head of corporate data processing approaches his job in an enlightened and objective manner.

Chapter 2

Management Participation in Day-to-Day Control

Many a new system has seriously overrun its target dates, and has cost several thousand pounds more than the original implementation estimates. It is not unusual to find applications which will cost, say, £50,000 left to develop in a haphazard environment. It is also common to hear of systems failing to provide their original benefits and exceeding their predicted operational budgets. These cases are responsible for the strong aversion which many senior managers have acquired towards computers. Whereas, in the mid 1960s, every captain of industry was eager to have his own computer, in the 1970s they seek to shed redundant hardware. Some companies have with benefit partially or wholly reverted to manual methods.

When a company's systems go wrong, the most instinctive reaction of top management is to change the computer manager and show a little less confidence in the data processing function. They may be justified in this attitude, but more often than not they should accept a large part of the blame themselves. Often the management remain very ignorant of what their computer can and cannot do, and in order not to expose their lack of knowledge, they have allowed the responsibility for computing to come to rest too far down the organisation. Even when top management does take an interest, as in establishing and approving prospective applications, it is often the case that no systematic follow up and monitoring plan exists.

The key to successful and profitable use of computers lies in the system adopted to justify each application and monitor it through design and implementation to operation. This chapter deals with this process and recommends a way in which management can retain control of their computer. It suggests a clear method for establishing objectives for each project, and a follow-up programme for review at key milestones in development.

However, before putting forward this fundamental and simple method for controlling projects, let us first examine some of the difficulties under which computer projects are developed. Perhaps in so doing we can

34

identify some of the most common errors made in management of computer projects.

The Difficulties of Scheduling

The most significant failing in controlling computer projects lies in identifying, at the beginning, what the project is all about. A job which starts with loosely defined objectives will soon run into trouble. Each line manager who has an interest in the system will seek to impose his own requirement on the project. This will take place throughout the life of the project, and the systems analyst will be faced with a constantly changing job requirement. Scheduled dates for completing phases of the work thus become a series of optimistic guesses. Far too many projects start with imprecise objectives, and this is one reason why computer projects run late. To produce an accurate schedule it is necessary to identify all the elements in a project, work out the resources required to carry out each element, ascertain what resources are available, and ascribe an elapsed time for each element accordingly. It should then be ascertained which elements can be progressed in parallel and which elements are dependent upon others and establish an overall schedule.

Yes, it is straightforward, and everyone should do it. But how many people actually do?

The problems are caused not because organisations fail to establish schedules – the real problem is that many users do not think through schedules in sufficient detail. They think that provided they have target dates and people working to them, then all will be well.

Let us illustrate the problem. Many organisations order computers before they have really designed the major systems that they intend to run on the computer. Usually this is done on the dubious basis that the whole system can be designed, programmed and established in operational mode during the manufacturer's lead time for delivery of the hardware.

In many cases, the decision to buy a particular configuration is taken on the basis of a report produced by the manufacturer's salesman after he has carried out a brief study of the organisation. In theory, the salesman, aided by systems engineers, will have satisfied himself that the configuration is right for his client's application, bearing in mind the volume and frequency of the data handled. However, it is unlikely that the application requirement has been specified in sufficient detail to be able to predict the time required to implement it.

All too often one reads on an order specification that 'the XYZ company has ordered a mixed disc/tape installation, with some terminals, for delivery in nine months' time – the main applications will be inventory control, sales accounting, and management information'.

Nine months or a year – these are magic time scales used by those of us who are afraid to admit to our colleagues and the world at large that we do not know. To be candid, it is very difficult for professional and capable data processing people to predict how long it will take to build a system

35

and get it operational. Take some typical stages in the creation of a system:

1 Define job requirement.
2 Produce system specification.
3 Produce program specifications.
4 Write and test programs.
5 Test complete system.
6 Educate and train users.
7 Trial operation.
8 Full operation.

Now it is quite feasible to establish all target dates at the beginnings, and management nearly always insists on it. Quite rightly, too, for we should have target dates for completing each of these activities, though it is highly unlikely that any of them will be kept to. If the system is moderately complex, we will not be able to predict how many programs have to be written until the end of Stage 2. Furthermore, the number of modules in each program and their complexity cannot be assessed until the end of Stage 3, and thus, until Stage 3 is completed, we cannot predict how long it will take to get to the end of Stage 4. Although I would insist on target dates for all stages of a project, I would not expect to consider those dates truly firm until a relevant preceding stage is completed.

Despite the fact that most of this is obvious and known by computer people and line management, they consistently fail to consider it when planning to introduce new systems. This lack of objectivity leads to the loss of confidence when the project dates slip by, and here is another of the fundamental reasons for people losing confidence in computers.

The reason why the dates set must be arbitrary is clear. A colleague and friend of mine, who is also one of the finest programmers and real-time project managers, explains it this way:

(a) No system is ever thought about until it is needed.
(b) No system designed is even started until it is too late, i.e. until the current system is operating in a very overloaded state.
(c) The management are so busy keeping current operations going that they haven't time to think through and define next year's requirement.
(d) No one can ever envisage waiting for more than a year for an improvement in the situation.

This diagnosis is not so cynical as it seems. These statements encapsulate a problem which many people fail to face when managing computer projects.

The Difficulty in Predicting Costs
So far we have identified a few simple milestones in the development of

a typical project, and simply suggested that we all recognise them for what they are. Of course, this will not instantly solve all the problems, but it does create an environment in which projects can be controlled effectively. Let us next look at project costs, which can be considered primarily under the following headings:

(a) Development costs.
(b) Operational costs.

To predict costs in development and to be able to minimise them requires the use of first-class estimating methods and project control techniques. The main areas of cost are:

(a) Man effort needed in defining job requirement and system specification.
(b) Manpower needed in programming computer procedures.
(c) Computer time required by programmers.
(d) Man effort needed in designing system trials.
(e) Man effort expended in training users.
(f) Effort expended by data processing staff and user departments in preparing and conducting system trials.

The operational costs of a system once it is running live include:

(g) A proportion (according to utilisation) of rental/depreciation, and maintenance costs of the equipment.
(h) Data control and preparation facilities.
(i) Stationery and documentation.
(j) Staff in user departments required to run the system.
(k) Maintenance work required from analysts and programmers.

If we identify for each of these items all the factors which contribute to minimising unnecessary costs, we will find that many factors are directly under the control of the data processing department. Since we are aiming in this book to deal with questions which can be more directly influenced by managers generally, I do not propose to go into such factors in detail. I will simply list those factors which the data processing manager is responsible for.

(a) The systems and programming teams must consist of professional and experienced staff.
(b) Consistent standards must exist for documentation and control of systems and programming work.
(c) Operations staff must be trained fully to utilise the expensive installations that they are responsible for.

(d) The data processing management must schedule work to ensure that the staff and equipment in the department are deployed efficiently.

(e) The necessary services needed by staff to create a stable environment for their projects must be provided.

Assuming that the data processing manager has done his job well, the line management has still a great deal of influence over the usefulness or otherwise of his department. If we analyse the main areas of cost given earlier in this section, it is apparent that we are always concerned with the efficient scheduling of skilled people and the expensive equipment that they utilise. Therefore management can play their part by :

(a) Making sure every project has defined objectives which are communicated to all users.

(b) That the project is justified on the basis of the benefits to the organisation considered against the development and operational costs.

(c) That key milestones are fixed to review progress and cost/benefits at frequent intervals in the life of the project.

(d) That reports and proposals produced by data processing people are promptly read and actioned.

(e) That members of management and user departments serve with data processing staff on project teams to design and plan implementation of systems.

(f) That projects are redesigned or abandoned if it becomes evident that the desired cost/benefits will not be achieved.

If a project is allowed to drag along without active participation by management, or to proceed in a loosely controlled fashion, the costs of the project will escalate. Man hours and machine time will be wasted in unnecessary debates about the project aims, and critical activities will remain uncompleted, thus delaying other dependent phases of the project. Let us now examine the sort of management participation that is necessary under each of these headings.

Defining Project Objectives
Too often, projects start with such generalised objectives that the systems analyst assigned to the task doesn't know where to begin. The danger is that he will carry out a lengthy investigation and eventually identify with the requirements of a particular line manager, who perhaps has a strong personality; or who perhaps shows a more overt interest in the analyst's work. The system which eventually materialises may therefore be useful, but not that which the organisation most needs.

I was once asked to develop an inventory control system for a spares organisation. The manager of the organisation wanted to improve his overall service to customers and to reduce inventory levels. It was a classic case, and he was right to expect improvements in both directions, but there were several possible ways of tackling the problem. A completely integrated system was eventually needed, but it was one which would take many years to develop. Some of the possible sub-systems required were:

(a) An order processing system for the central store.
(b) An order processing system for satellite depots.
(c) A provisioning system for kits compiled to a determined programme.
(d) A forecasting system for ordering replacement parts.
(e) An accurate stock recording system.
(f) An accurate auditing and accounting system.
(g) A system to suggest optimum distribution of materials to depots.

This project began in an ill co-ordinated manner with various department heads applying pressure to start on their problem first. Eventually the organisation manager was persuaded to commission an operational investigation which suggested the areas where the most worthwhile benefits could be achieved. Two of the sub-systems were therefore chosen for immediate development, and others followed later. Until this step was taken a great deal of time and effort was wasted.

Systems are very rarely complete in themselves, but nearly always impinge upon other systems, and it is therefore difficult to delineate the boundaries of each project. I would suggest that a sound method of beginning a project would include the following stages:

(a) Initial identification of the problem by management with aims expressed in economic terms.
(b) If necessary, a feasibility study to identify the functions covered and techniques to be adopted.
(c) A job requirement specification to provide terms of reference for the analysis phase.

These steps can be completed quickly, and the level of detail required may depend on the nature of the problem – sometimes a detailed feasibility report is not necessary.

The objective setting should be done under the control of, and with the approval of, the director or executive responsible for the division concerned, and the other executives and staff in the division should be consulted and informed. Perhaps the best solution is to set up a small working party, under the chairmanship of the director concerned, which will carry out the following tasks:

(a) Prepare and ratify the economic aims.
(b) Seek support from other units.
(c) Commission specific studies to ascertain feasibility.
(d) Agree cost benefits and prepare development budgets.

39

(e) Approve system development plan and establish project management structure.
(f) Monitor development at key milestones.
(g) Approve diversions from plan or budget.
(h) Monitor economic achievements.

A committee with these terms of reference is sometimes called a *steering committee*; this title somehow implies guidance rather than control, and I therefore prefer *systems management committee.*

Establishing Cost/Benefits

Computer departments do not generate profits in their own right, yet, as a cost centre, a computer department may represent between 1 per cent and 2 per cent of the organisation's turnover. Thus a considerable degree of control needs to be exercised over the total volume of data processing expenditure, and the deployment of the resources concerned .

Each computer project should be expected to produce a return equivalent to the return expected of other types of investment within the organisation. What is more, this return must be produced each year for as long as the system operates. It is most likely that suitable investment opportunities will be found only in the major operational units of the organisation.

It is one of the great weaknesses in the management of computing activity that so few organisations have evolved a methodical approach to the identification and evaluation of opportunities. I have therefore devoted the whole of Chapter 3 to a discussion of this topic. It is, however, worthwhile at this juncture to note the following points.

Some of the most disastrous computing failures have occurred with long-range investments, upon projects which have attempted the great leap forward. It is nowadays unfashionable to invest in such projects, even though the general level of technology is more credible than heretofore. This should not necessarily mean that no long-range benefits are sought, but is inclined towards a more practical strategy where such benefits are obtained via short-term and medium-term investments, each providing benefits in their own right.

In an ideal situation, the systems analysts and the line management must collaborate in assessing the cost/benefits of any project: the user management being mainly responsible for assessing the benefits and the systems people the costs of system development and operation of the system subsequently.

A diagram showing typical cost/benefit curves is given in Figure 4.1, page 82. Here we see that the costs are highest when the development work is being done, and that the benefits enter into the picture as parts of the system go operational, eventually overtaking the total costs. The volume of the benefits and the point at which the investment is returned is important.

The selection of projects should always be undertaken with the aid of such an analysis, and it is also important not to consider particular projects in isolation, since even more significant returns may be achieved by investing in an alternative project.

Project Management Structure

As we have seen earlier in this chapter, it is not always possible to forecast at the beginning of a project precisely what the development and operational costs of a system will be. Neither is it easy to forecast benefits with confidence. Thus it is necessary constantly to monitor what happens during the project to ascertain whether any circumstances arise which modify the original economic aims. The important issues to be kept under observation include:

(a) Technological difficulties which may effect the subsequent performance of the system.
(b) Changes in schedule which may cause the completion to go beyond a critical deadline.
(c) Increase in development cost.
(d) Increase in forecast operational costs for the future system.
(e) Changes in the business environment which may modify the original objectives.

This monitoring role should be performed by the chief executives of the divisions concerned (hereafter referred to as *senior management*): to whom the line management and data processing management will have to report at regular intervals. The interval between senior management review meetings must be relatively short, and certainly never more than two months.

At more frequent intervals, project management meetings on detailed aspects of the project should take place involving line staff and data processing staff. The following overall pattern should be established:

Every two months: Senior management review progress and problems arising.
Every month: Project management (line and data processing management) review progress and problems and set tasks and agree timescales and resources for project teams.
Every week: Team leaders evaluate tasks, schedule team members, monitor progress and identify problems arising.

The main functions performed by each of these three levels of project management are given in Figure 2.1.

This is not a novel approach to project management, but it is common for organisations to fail in their attempts to carry it out. The failings usually stem from senior executives setting the wrong style and tone for such meetings, or else are caused by them not keeping to a regular pattern of meetings.

Figure 2.1 *Functions of management related to a project.*

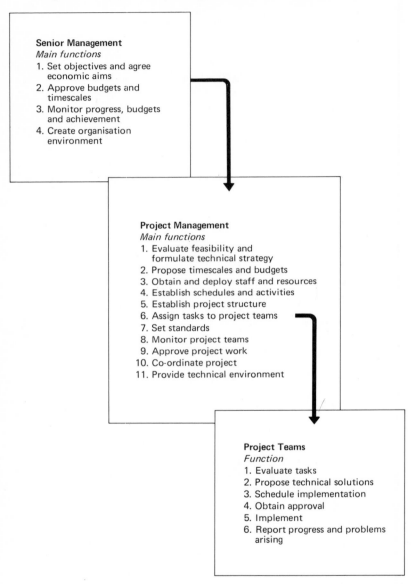

Senior Management
Main functions
1. Set objectives and agree economic aims
2. Approve budgets and timescales
3. Monitor progress, budgets and achievement
4. Create organisation environment

Project Management
Main functions
1. Evaluate feasibility and formulate technical strategy
2. Propose timescales and budgets
3. Obtain and deploy staff and resources
4. Establish schedules and activities
5. Establish project structure
6. Assign tasks to project teams
7. Set standards
8. Monitor project teams
9. Approve project work
10. Co-ordinate project
11. Provide technical environment

Project Teams
Function
1. Evaluate tasks
2. Propose technical solutions
3. Schedule implementation
4. Obtain approval
5. Implement
6. Report progress and problems arising

The structure of the project management meetings should be such that all departments committed to the implementation of the system are represented. Each representative must be prepared to:

(a) Report progress against his targets.
(b) Identify any problems or obstacles to progress.
(c) Propose solutions to problems.

The atmosphere must be such that objective discussions take place and decisions are taken. If this style can be set for the meetings at each level, it will greatly influence the success of the project.

The Importance of Milestones

To provide a framework against which to monitor the progress of the project, it is also essential to establish control points or milestones. All activities which are essential to achieving each milestone should be identified and evaluated by the relevant qualified staff. Reporting for each major activity should then include, as a minimum:

(a) Target completion date.
(b) Estimated total effort needed.
(c) Percentage completed to date.
(d) Forecast completion date.
(e) Forecast effort required to complete.
(f) Original cost estimate.
(g) Revised cost estimate.

The allowed time between milestones set for a project should be of relatively short duration; otherwise too much time and effort can be lost before the project management can focus upon the issues concerned. At the team leader level, where many detailed activities have to be monitored and controlled, the allowed time for some of these activities may be one or two days. The project management should expect to receive detailed reports from team leaders on the activities against detailed schedules which have been agreed.

Figure 2.2 suggests some major milestones which should provide opportunities for the project management to review technical strategies and budgets, and also allow the senior management to reassess the economic potential and general progress of the project. This illustration also shows, by contrast, examples of detailed project activities which will be used by the project management and individual teams to monitor progress in finer detail.

The milestones chosen for control purposes in reporting to each level of project management must be pertinent to the reviewing members. For example, the senior management should expect to exert particular control over the following stages of the project:

(a) The agreement of objectives and economic aims.
(b) Review and approval of the feasibility study.

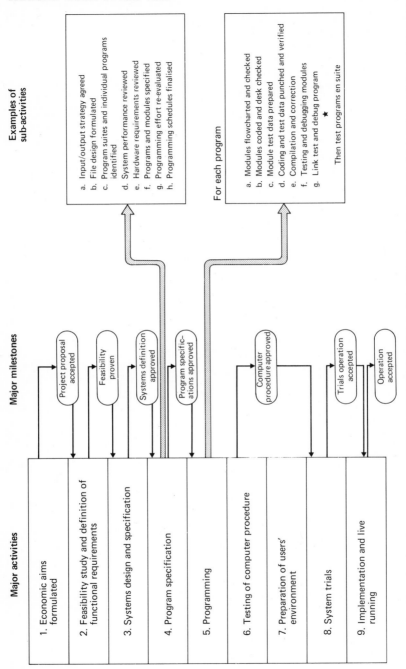

Major activities

1. Economic aims formulated

2. Feasibility study and definition of functional requirements

3. Systems design and specification

4. Program specification

5. Programming

6. Testing of computer procedure

7. Preparation of users' environment

8. System trials

9. Implementation and live running

Major milestones

Project proposal accepted

Feasibility proven

Systems definition approved

Program specific-ations approved

Computer procedure approved

Trials operation accepted

Operation accepted

Examples of sub-activities

a. Input/output strategy agreed
b. File design formulated
c. Program suites and individual programs identified
d. System performance reviewed
e. Hardware requirements reviewed
f. Programs and modules specified
g. Programming effort re-evaluated
h. Programming schedules finalised

For each program

a. Modules flowcharted and checked
b. Modules coded and desk checked
c. Module test data prepared
d. Coding and test data punched and verified
e. Compilation and correction
f. Testing and debugging modules
g. Link test and debug program
★
Then test programs en suite

Figure 2.2 *Project activities and major milestones.*

(c) Approval of system design and the forecast costs and timescale of implementation.

(d) Regular review over implementation and control over changes in objectives and in budgets.

The senior management team may well feel that the continuing meetings to review implementation do not warrant so much of their attention as do the earlier objective setting activities. This is a mistaken attitude. Their critical approval of the project is essential to its success, and their influence and interest throughout will permit an objective reassessment of the project at key milestones.

The project itself may well be divided into subsidiary activities requiring small teams to be set up involving line and data processing staff. Each project task will have specific terms of reference and the task group will be asked to complete it within a relatively short timescale.

Project Tasks

So far, I have identified the major activities in each complete project and recommended a project structure involving the various levels of management in the control of the overall project. It is also important that the participation of management and staff in user departments be obtained in carrying out the detailed tasks of designing and implementing the system. These tasks will vary in nature according to the stage of the project, but the same formal methods can be used to control them. The following criteria should be observed:

(a) Each task should have formal terms of reference to achieve a specific objective.

(b) The task group should consist of both data processing staff and relevant staff from line departments.

(c) The group should report on progress, problems and achievements to the project management level.

(d) The task should be one which can be achieved in a relatively short duration, e.g. four weeks.

(e) The task group should meet frequently, e.g. weekly.

(f) The task group should be led by a chairman who will control meetings.

(g) Individual members of the task group should be assigned to investigate specific matters and report back to the group.

(h) It should be recognised that members of the task group will need to be free from some of their routine commitments.

Some examples of individual tasks which can be sensibly conducted in this way include:

(a) The design of a specific procedure.

(b) The specification of system outputs.

45

(c) The creation and conversion of a file.
(d) Designing a system trial plan.
(e) Planning the implementation of changeover to live running a system.
(f) Design of specific documents.
(g) The planning of validation and data correction procedures.

The benefit of tackling such activities in this way is that it gets data processing staff and line staff working together on the resolution of problems, thus creating better team spirit in the organisation and avoiding the situation where the eventual users of the system feel that they have not been consulted. In some cases, it may be best to make a line manager responsible as chairman of a particular project task; in another case, a systems analyst may be appropriate. The members of a project team will be people best able to deal with the subject concerned, and this may involve junior staff from line departments. The use of task groups rather than a single individual may make some people apprehensive of the efficiency of the method, but in practice it is found that work is more easily controlled and monitored in this way. More important is the sense of involvement which line departments will have in the system. They will consider the system to be largely of their own design and making if they have been involved through the many project teams necessary to implement the system.

SUMMARY OF CHAPTER 2

In this chapter, I have concentrated on some simple and fundamental issues which will create a stable environment for the effective creation and implementation of information systems. The following check-list summarises the main points made in this chapter, and can be used to examine the methods adopted by organisations to implement particular systems:

1   Each project must start with an objective.
2   The objective must be agreed by the senior management.
3   The objective must be formally conveyed to all those concerned.
4   There has to be a defined economic aim expressed in the objective.
5   A preliminary study may need to be conducted to establish the real potential of achieving the economic aim.
6   An attempt should be made to predict development costs and future operational costs.
7   Key milestones must be identified to review these costs.
8   A formal cost/benefit analysis should be carried out.
9   The original cost/benefit analysis must be checked at key milestones.
10   A system development plan and budget should be compiled.
11   The project management structure should allow for control and monitoring of achievements by the senior management.
12   A schedule with target dates should be established.

13 The schedule must include all the principal activities which have to be completed.

14 The target dates should be flexible in that they can be revised as the requirement is evaluated at each key milestone.

15 The line management must understand the importance of the activities in the schedule and the milestones.

16 The project management team should be representative of relevant data processing and line management functions.

17 Individual project teams with clear terms of reference should be set up to carry out particular tasks.

18 The various levels of management should review the project frequently, e.g.

Senior management: every two months
Project management: monthly
Project teams: weekly

19 *Detailed* progress information should be reported.

20 Progress reports have to be critically examined to identify causes for slippage and whether corrective action has to be taken.

21 Sensible forecasts of likely completion must be included in progress reports.

22 Action must be taken to help project teams when they identify factors delaying their work.

23 All project meetings and formal reviews must be conducted in an objective manner.

24 Each project review should establish whether the investment in the project is likely to return the anticipated benefits within the desired timescale.

25 If the project review shows that worthwhile benefits will not be achieved, then consider abandoning the project.

Chapter 3

Project Control: The Key to Saving Money

In Chapter 2 we discussed the part which different levels of management should take in establishing an environment for controlling their data processing activity. Now we shall examine some of the common errors which occur in preparing for and implementing individual projects. I have generally assumed in this chapter that we are considering a large dedicated project which requires to be planned and executed from the beginning. However, the principles described apply to any project.

Time is always the enemy of a successful project, and we have stressed the importance of a realistic approach to establishing the time and resources needed to achieve the various milestones in project development. However, if the impression has been given that usually insufficient time is allowed for implementation, we must also show the other side of the coin . . . . Time is very often wasted because problems are not anticipated and dealt with before they become critical.

On small projects, it is possible to depend on individuals and ad hoc actions to overcome crises. On large projects, this is not satisfactory. Problems must be anticipated, and avoiding action has to be taken to prevent a serious disruption of the schedule. It is unfortunately true that schedules are frequently produced on the assumption that everything will go well. This attitude prevails despite the circumstantial evidence which exists to prove that things usually do not go according to plan.

Perhaps there is an infectious optimism which afflicts all computer people when they initially schedule a project. Also it is true that we generally fail to recognise all the potential problem areas, and that the control systems which we adopt in project development do not allow us to foresee difficulties until we have been run over by them. The standard reaction to such difficulties is to pour in more effort.

The expert project managers in the industry would describe this malaise as a case of 'too little and too late'. It certainly explains many of the failures which are encountered. Furthermore, it can be true that pouring resources into a late project can overburden the management and communication structure, in which case the phrase 'too much and too late' seems appropriate.

In this chapter we will identify, in more detail, an approach which will avoid this condition.

PREPARING FOR A PROJECT

Reviewing the Requirement

A large project will usually start off with a requirement specification which has perhaps been produced by a small team. When the decision is taken to go ahead with the project, it is probable that there has been a significant delay since the specification was first produced. There may also have been much discussion and negotiation about the requirement, and it is probable that, in the process, changes will have been necessary. The first step before commencing any detailed design work should therefore be a further review of the requirement specification by the systems designers to ensure that no omissions or inconsistencies exist. Time must be allowed for this, and it should not be considered a luxury. Errors identified at this stage will be less costly than errors discovered later.

Determining Standards

Before commencing the detailed design work, it will also be necessary to specify some technical standards and to establish formal methods of communication for the project. On very large projects, the format and content of all specification documents, their distribution and authorisation may have to be deliberately established. A procedure for controlling changes to specifications and rules for authorising and acting upon change notices has to be formulated. These activities will consume time, and it is essential that they are organised before large numbers of people are employed on the project. A continuing effort may be required throughout the project by people whose role it is to administer these communication channels. Such effort should be included in the budget for the project.

Technical Preparations

Even on relatively small projects, it may be necessary to provide special technical facilities for developing and testing the application. The provision of such software as module testers, simulators and test file generators may be a vital activity which will need to be planned with care, and again allowances for the production or acquisition of such facilities must be included in the project schedule. It is also important to include time for the familiarisation of personnel with any new techniques, facilities or standards.

Activities such as these, designed to guarantee more effective implementation of the system, can sometimes be developed in parallel with the design stage of the system. It is, however, most important to avoid starting the programming work until such facilities as are needed are available. The induction of programming staff can then be organised so that they can be prepared to operate in the required environment.

Supporting Services

In preparation for the programming and testing phases of the development, it is also essential to ensure that adequate supporting services are available, e.g. data preparation, computer time, transportation of work to and from the computer, and perhaps terminals for program development work. A programmer may well need access to computer time two or three times a day in order to maintain momentum at key points in the project, and a typing service will be needed to maintain the output of documentation by systems analysts. Too often one observes that these everyday items get overlooked and that consequently the productivity and morale of the project staff are affected.

Project Control Methods

The project schedule will start off as a series of standard milestones, and become expanded into more detail as various phases of the project are completed and more information about subsequent stages become available. The computer staff responsible for the project will require to break these activities into great detail as sub-activities in order to monitor technical progress of the project. Importance has to be placed on monitoring each sub-activity closely enough to observe slippages within a few days of their occurrence; and this implies that a sub-activity should not last more than, say, ten days. For example, the sub-activities involved in controlling the writing of a particular program might be as follows, with the time allowed (in days) indicated in the right-hand column:

Study specification of program	2
Plan program structure and approach	$\frac{1}{2}$
Flowchart program	1
Flowchart detailed logic of module*	$\frac{1}{2}$
Check module flowchart*	$\frac{1}{2}$
Code module and desk check*	2
Punch module*	$\frac{1}{2}$
Compile module and correct coding errors*	1
Design test data*	4
Create new files*	2
Individually test modules*	3
Correct logic errors*	3
Prepare program test data	3
Link-test modules	2
Correct errors	3
Obtain approval of results	1
Complete documentation	3

(*For each module of the program.)

50

This schedule, for developing a single program, will take more than six working weeks, and adding a contingency to allow for unscheduled problems such as sickness, will cause the elapsed time to extend to seven weeks. It is not so easy to break other phases of project development into such detail as in program development, but it can and must be attempted.

It is not prudent to monitor progress of sub-activities less frequently than once a week. At each review the progress to date has to be recorded. Any delays must be recognised, and a forecast of the likely completion dates of subsequent stages of activity, be obtained. Problems encountered by project staff must be dealt with by providing any necessary help and facilities to overcome them and to keep the activity progressing in accordance with the schedule.

This type of control is, of course, the responsibility of the computer personnel forming the project staff. However, the management of the user organisation should be familiar with the primary network and the activities therein, and should monitor progress at least once a month in accordance with the general principles described above.

By adopting a rigorous approach to project control, it is possible to compensate for the fallibility which everyone experiences in estimating the amount of work entailed in developing a new system. There are many systems of project control in use today; the main objective is to provide accurate and timely information to enable decisions to be taken about the deployment of resources to meet the cost and time constraints placed upon the project.

I have included as an annex to this chapter an extract from a Project Management Standard used by Dataskil to control the development of applications. This extract explains clearly the principles behind the method and gives examples of the documentation used in practice to collect and present information.

PERT Networks

Computerised systems of project management exist and, among these, various forms of PERT (project evaluation and review technique) provide a very effective system for project control; but it must also be remembered that it takes time and effort to administer such systems successfully. A great deal of information must be collected accurately to update the network on each occasion before producing a new printout.

If this process is not efficiently executed, the results of any new schedule may be inaccurate, or may be obtained too late to be of effective use in taking controlling action.

To be effective, the PERT network must embrace all activities or suspected activities. In particular, the network must include all the external dependencies which are under control of the eventual users of the system. Very often one finds that PERT networks are set up to embrace all the detailed activities of the computer side of project development, but the key external dependencies are unfortunately omitted.

51

PERT is very important on any project entailing more than, say, a hundred activities, but it may be an expensive and useless overhead if the project management group do not use the results with firmness and flexibility. A PERT run can allow the evaluation of the effects of different resource loadings, enabling the management to assess the benefit that different actions may have. For example, one can assume that infinite resources are available and ascertain the earliest possible completion date; also one can set specific target dates and ascertain the likely resource requirements. Judgement will always need to be applied to assess whether the answers that PERT provides are practical in the prevailing circumstances. It is no good planning to apply staff to a project if they are not available, or not trained in the correct skills. Increasing human resources on a technical project also implies increasing supervision and co-ordinating staff to make sure that communication and control remain effective.

Whether PERT or some other manual method for charting and monitoring progress is adopted for project control, the important factor will remain the attitude of the management to the information that the system provides. Flexibility and decisiveness combined with a sound judgement are all-important.

Staffing the Project
Having established an initial network, plans must be laid to develop the staffing of the project and to formulate a plan for the development of the organisation.

Project teams cannot be created overnight, but projects, once they have been approved, are usually required to start up rapidly. Thus there is a need to obtain a wide variety of skills at short notice. This will present problems which may well justify the temporary creation of a special unit to recruit staff and allocate them to different parts of the project.

To succeed in computing, there is one golden rule : always make sure that projects are staffed with truly *experienced* and *professional* people in all *key* situations.

The needs of the project have to be carefully analysed and the skills of the available staff matched against these needs. The tasks should be defined and the project teams structured to recognise the qualities that you can expect to find in individuals.

Personnel joining the project will need to be aware of the total environment in which they will be operating, and this will entail indoctrination in the commercial, technical and administrative background.

The staff loading for the project will have to be continually reviewed at successive milestones in the project, and a flexible attitude has to be created to allow the project structure to be tuned to the requirements of the job at different phases of development.

Project Organisation
The aim in creating an organisation structure is to enable the project to be

completed within the prescribed timescale and cost. The problem which arises in many projects is that the time and money allocated to complete the task begin to run out. The tendency in these circumstances is to ignore some tasks and focus attention on those which seem most important, with the result that the tasks which are deferred become urgent sooner or later. It is therefore important to attempt the following:

(a) To foresee all the tasks which require to be undertaken.
(b) To allow reasonable contingency for the unexpected.
(c) To allocate tasks to individuals who will have sole responsibility for completing them.

This last requirement is one of the key objectives of the organisation structure.

There is a significant danger in the allocation of work to project staff: care must be taken not to overload individuals and yet, on the other hand, not to set a slack tempo throughout the project. Some tasks may not be full-time occupations, and it may be sensible to allocate more than one such task to a member of the team. Never split the responsibility for a task.

It is also important to give people the kind of work for which they have an aptitude, and jobs should not be defined as whole tasks if they require combinations of qualities not normally found in individuals. There is a particular danger in the computer industry of arranging career progressions so that all technical people must aspire to become managers. This frequently leads to the situation where a technically sound individual finds himself having to make managerial and commercial judgements which he does not enjoy or carry through.

There is a real case for divorcing many of the technical and administrative functions in creating the organisation. (As a side-issue, it is worth noting that salary progressions for technical staff should be at least as good as their project managers.)

Ideally, the key management positions should be staffed with people who have considerable technical and managerial ability. This combination of skills is not so rare as it used to be in the computer industry.

An organisation chart for the commencement of a project is shown in Figure 3.1. It can be compared with one shown later in Figure 3.2, which reflects the changed structure required for a later development phase of the project. This is illustrative of the need for flexibility in tuning the organisation to reflect the project requirements. The major functions identified in these illustrations apply to small projects as well as large ones. For example, the systems trials controller in Figure 3.2 could perform all the functions described on his own, but in a very large project he may have two or three systems analysts planning the trials strategy and supervising the trials as well as several clerks at some stage for the preparation of test data.

53

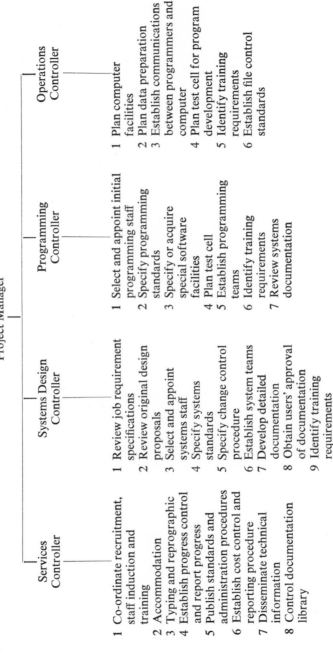

Figure 3.1 *Initial organisation of a project.*

Project Manager

Services Controller

1 Co-ordinate recruitment, staff induction and training
2 Accommodation
3 Typing and reprographic
4 Establish progress control and report progress
5 Publish standards and administration procedures
6 Establish cost control and reporting procedure
7 Disseminate technical information
8 Control documentation library

Systems Design Controller

1 Review job requirement specifications
2 Review original design proposals
3 Select and appoint systems staff
4 Specify systems standards
5 Specify change control procedure
6 Establish system teams
7 Develop detailed documentation
8 Obtain users' approval of documentation
9 Identify training requirements

Programming Controller

1 Select and appoint initial programming staff
2 Specify programming standards
3 Specify or acquire special software facilities
4 Plan test cell
5 Establish programming teams
6 Identify training requirements
7 Review systems documentation

Operations Controller

1 Plan computer facilities
2 Plan data preparation
3 Establish communications between programmers and computer
4 Plan test cell for program development
5 Identify training requirements
6 Establish file control standards

Figure 3.2 *Project organisation for design stage.*

Project Manager

Services Controller	Systems Trials Controller	Systems Design Controller	Programming Controller	Operations Controller
As for 3.1 plus:	1 Review design proposals	1 Develop suite test data	1 Set up special facilities	1 Operate computer facilities
1 Maintenance of PERT	2 Prepare performance estimates	2 Begin testing program suites	2 Develop program specifications	2 Operate data preparation facilities
2 Cost and progress reports	3 Assist in evaluating and approving amendments	3 Co-ordinate provision of external requirements	3 Develop and test programs	3 Control magnetic media
	4 Organise preparation of total-system test data	4 User liaison and education	4 Link programs and test en suite	4 Plan computer environment for full system operation
	5 Prepare users for participation in total-system trials	5 Evaluate amendment requests	5 Participate in evaluation and approval of amendment requests	
	6 Conduct total-system trials	6 Amend systems documentation	6 Document programs	
	7 Propose system changes	7 Approve completion of program suites	7 Develop program library	
	8 Approve system for live implementation	8 Develop final implementation plans		

55

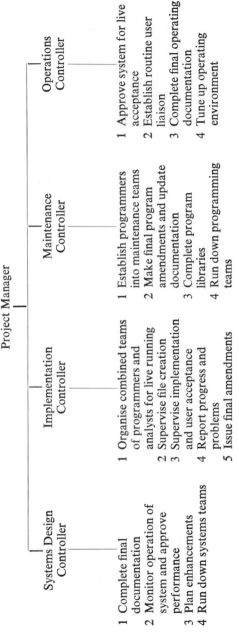

Figure 3.3 *Project organisation for final implementation.*

Project Manager

Systems Design Controller

1 Complete final documentation
2 Monitor operation of system and approve performance
3 Plan enhancements
4 Run down systems teams

Implementation Controller

1 Organise combined teams of programmers and analysts for live running
2 Supervise file creation
3 Supervise implementation and user acceptance
4 Report progress and problems
5 Issue final amendments

Maintenance Controller

1 Establish programmers into maintenance teams
2 Make final program amendments and update documentation
3 Complete program libraries
4 Run down programming teams

Operations Controller

1 Approve system for live acceptance
2 Establish routine user liaison
3 Complete final operating documentation
4 Tune up operating environment

Figure 3.3 shows the organisation to complete the project.

The final stages of development will probably require some of the systems and programming staff to be combined into teams whose task it will be to carry out the 'cut-over' to live running. These teams may be required to make last-minute amendments to programs to keep the system live, but this will be minimised if time has been taken to operate a full and searching trial of the system. Meanwhile, the original programming group will be organising itself into maintenance units to support the live system, while the systems group complete the final documentation and plan future enhancements.

None of the functions listed in the organisational charts accompanying this chapter can be treated lightly. Even on a small project, the activities defined here must be considered in the project schedule. The activities must also be allocated to project members who have the relevant skills and time available to execute them.

The Importance of Review Stages

In the desire to keep projects moving along crisply to completion there is a tendency to begin one phase of the project as soon as, if not before, the preceding stage is completed. The most common example of this condition is the urge to begin programming before system design is completed. However, if the design has not been sufficiently advanced before programming commences there is a probability that programming resources will be committed to a bad design and that there will be a considerable loss of management control as the change control procedure is overburdened with amendments. To safeguard against this condition it is necessary to build formal review stages into the project, as shown in Figure 3.4 The management should resist the natural inclination to use the time thus allotted as a contingency to recover ground lost elsewhere on the project.

Figure 3.4   *Stages for project review*

1 Document system objectives
               Review objectives
2 Specify job requirements
               Review requirements
3 Produce outline design proposal
               Review design proposal
4 Document detailed system design
               Review detailed system design
5 Produce and publish program specifications
               Review program specifications
6 Produce testing strategy
               Review testing strategy
7 Prepare user training programme
               Review training programme
8 Plan for implementation
               Review implementation plans

57

A review is particularly important at any milestone which involves the commitment to technical strategies, or which precedes a stage entailing the deployment of resources on a large scale. The review itself is really an opportunity to tidy up the preceding stage, and is best done by a member of the team who has not been involved in the preceding work. The following should form the basis of each review:

(a) Evaluation of system performance.
(b) Efficacy of design concepts.
(c) Project timescales and costs.
(d) Staff requirements.
(e) Cohesiveness of overall design.

Man-Effort versus Progress

One of the curious attitudes which systems and programming people exhibit is the tendency to confuse effort with achievement. By this I mean that we assume that putting more effort into a project will bring about a faster rate of progress. This is not necessarily a valid or reasonable assumption. Nevertheless we often find systems and programming managers compelled by circumstances to think of their projects as consisting solely of man-weeks of effort which can be parcelled out to staff as required to achieve a desired completion date.

An unconsidered factor is the communication which will be necessary among the project team to realise the full efficiency of each member. There is a diminishing return associated with an increase in the number of people on a particular task. It is very difficult to account for this communication overhead, but it consists of the following elements:

(a) General training and awareness of the aims, standards and techniques to be adopted in the project.
(b) A continuing dialogue between members of the team who are working on sub-tasks which must be co-ordinated.

Communication can be relatively informal if the team is small (say three or four people), but must be formally documented and organised where more people are involved. Since this communication is brought about by the need to tell individual team members what is required of them, it follows that supervisory effort has to be increased to monitor that the communication has been understood and the requirements correctly implemented.

An example of the implications for project organisation is shown in Figure 3.5. Here we first assume that a project is planned to be executed using five people, one of whom is the project leader. The leader can, if necessary, communicate with and monitor the work of all members of his team, or he may choose to deal through the two senior programmers.

Now, if the project falls behind schedule, in the program specification stage, for example, the obvious way to make up time will be to apply more programmers in program development. In the example eleven people have been put into the project with an increase in supervisory effort and a consequent enlargement of the communication overhead.

Figure 3.5   *Increasing the man-effort in a project.*

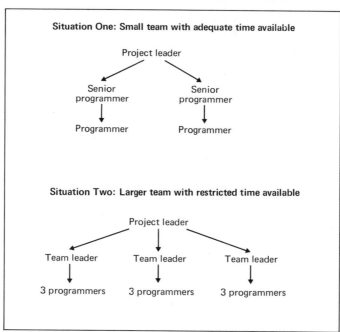

It is possible that the project leader could directly control more programmers. The deciding factor is whether, in practice, he is able to keep up with their work and correct their mistakes and misunderstandings before these cause serious delays. Eventually, the different programs and modules will have to be integrated into a coherent system, and one wrongly conceived module may cause delays out of all proportion to the effort originally needed to get it right.

Another factor which diminishes the return associated with increased effort is the sequential nature of many sub-tasks forming a project. This is particularly evident in the program testing and linking phases of a project.

The testing of software is a notoriously difficult process to forecast accurately. The nature and variety of errors encountered defies any attempt to establish standard units of work for scheduling this phase of the project. Usually this process is most efficiently executed if a testing plan is established to enable individual modules and programs to be care-

59

fully tested in simulated conditions before being integrated to form the total system. The team should be trimmed to a minimum number of staff for this final phase, each of whom should be thoroughly knowledgeable of the overall system and able to turn his hands to any activity needed. It is usually helpful to build up history to evaluate the time spent in various stages of project development and to question any proposed schedules against previous experience. It is not very encouraging to find out that, by increasing effort, one is increasing the problems in implementation. As a general rule, it pays to keep the project team small and increase efficiency and output by making sure that external causes of delays are identified and eliminated. The product will ultimately deteriorate and fail to yield the desired benefits if corners are cut and pressure is applied unthinkingly to reach an unrealistic target date.

The summary to this chapter gives the essential points which will result in good project control and give a reasonable chance of achieving a good product on time.

SUMMARY OF CHAPTER 3

In Chapter 3 we have identified some of the key issues to be considered in setting up a development project. The main points of the chapter are sum-marised below. A more detailed standard for project control is included in an annex to this chapter.

1   Time is wasted, and money lost, if problems cannot be anticipated before they create critical situations.
2   Resources are not unlimited and cannot be effectively applied at short notice to overcome crises.
3   Increasing the manpower on a project may entail increasing the manage-ment and communication overhead if the resources are to be efficiently applied to the project.
4   Before commencing a new phase of a project, the results of the pre-ceding phase should be reviewed to ascertain errors and omissions, and to assess the aptness of previous thinking in the current circumstances.
5   Standards for design work and for documentation at intermediate and final stages must be formulated before design work gets under way.
6   A change control procedure should be established.
7   All technical aids and facilities needed to develop the project should be foreseen.
8   Training and induction plans should be created for new staff joining a project.
9   Adequate supporting services must exist.
10   A project control method must be adopted to monitor progress and enable effective decisions to be made. (A method of documentation is described in the annex to this chapter.)

60

11   The project should be subdivided into activities and sub-activities of short duration.

12   Progress and problems encountered in completing these activities to schedule must be reviewed at short intervals.

13   Problems encountered must be dealt with objectively and energetically.

14   Computerised systems of project control exist, among which various forms of PERT are available and permit a high degree of flexibility.

15   Staff assigned to a project must be sufficiently skilled to carry out the tasks assigned. Training and indoctrination may be required to prepare them for participation in the project.

16   Tasks should be allocated to individuals who will have responsibility for completing them and reporting progress.

17   The organisation structure should be capable of adaptation as the project develops.

18   There should be a formal review of the technical and economic strategies at key milestones in project development.

19   A new stage must not start until such a review has been completed to include:

    (a)   System performance.
    (b)   Design concepts.
    (c)   Project timescales and costs.
    (d)   Staff requirements.
    (e)   Overall cohesiveness of the design.

20   There may be a diminishing return in applying manpower to a project; a late project can be further delayed by the indiscriminate provision of more staff.

Annex to Chapter 3:

Extract from the Dataskil Project Management Manual

This annex contains an extract from a Project Management Manual used by Dataskil Limited, a software house subsidiary of International Computers Limited. It contains a description of a simple management system which is used successfully to control major software projects where the total cost of the project in terms of man-effort alone might approach or exceed £100,000.

I have included this extract unedited, since it concisely describes the basic control mechanism used without requiring any specialised knowledge on the part of the reader. It is a deceptively simple system to set up and adopt, yet it yields very significant benefits in the hands of managers who display the right attitude to monitoring and controlling activities. The annex makes references to several sections of the Dataskil standards manual, but the extract included here is taken from Sections 1 and 2 only.

This extract from the Project Management Manual and the Control Charts are reproduced here with the kind permission of Dataskil.

1 INTRODUCTION

1.1 WHAT IS A COMPUTER PROJECT?

It can be justifiably argued that any work which involves a computer-based technique can be defined as a computer project. Thus a computer project could be anything from programmer hire to the design and implementation of a large complex computer system. In fact it doesn't much matter what the definition is, what is important is that any company that carries out computer projects should have a defined project management structure which facilitates the effective management of the whole range of projects it is likely to tackle.

1.2 WHAT IS A PROJECT MANAGEMENT STRUCTURE?

Purpose
The purpose of a project management structure is to provide information

which will enable the person or persons responsible for a project to control it, to make decisions based on the most accurate possible information and to pass accurate information to higher management which can be used to make financial and marketing policies and decisions. Of course the decisions made may be bad, but they will not be bad due to a lack of accurate information.

People succeed not systems

Projects are and always will be only as good as the people who staff them. A project management structure will highlight poorly managed projects in time for them to be saved from disaster. However, a project management structure can only turn on the red light, it cannot take the required action. People must make the decisions and take the actions.

Not a constraint

A project management structure is *not* a set of standards which constrain people, it is a structure which can be used to obtain information with which to make more effective decisions and to carry out effective control. It also provides a flexibility which enables anyone familiar with the project management structure to take over a project with the minimum of disruption.

Not a static state

To be dogmatic about a particular project management structure is to be short-sighted. With the rapidity that changes take place within the business world and the computer industry the structure should always be evolving and being modified to reflect these changes. It would, however, be a disaster to change the structure from day to day. What is required is a six-monthly review at which time the appropriateness of the structure is reviewed and any necessary changes made. These changes must be well documented and distributed to all concerned.

1.3 WHO IS A PROJECT MANAGER?

The person who is responsible for the day-to-day management of any project can be defined as the project manager. The management responsibility could be for anything from two programmers working on a customer site to a large project involving many analysts and programmers.

Clearly the skills required to perform these differing management functions vary considerably. The simplest project will carry project manager responsibility, but will not require the use of all of the project management skills. The more complex projects will require both project manager responsibility and the full range of project management skills. This situation will satisfy the needs of both the staff and the company, provided it is known which of the skills the developing project manager still requires to learn or develop and time is made available to do so. Project managers are best developed through appropriate courses backed by a well-orientated practical experience.

2 THE PROJECT MANAGEMENT STRUCTURE

2.1 PERSONNEL STRUCTURE

On all projects the project manager will be totally responsible for the project and all reporting to branch managers or higher management will be done through the project manager. In the most simplified form, the personnel structure of a project will be as shown below in A. The project staff could be anything from say 2 to 200 people. A 'complete' project would probably have a structure similar to that shown in either B or C.

In the ideal situation, the project manager will be involved from the initial inquiry to the completion of the project. Although it is hoped that this will often occur in the real situation, it will sometimes not, and therefore any good project management structure must make allowances for personnel changes, including that of project manager. It will be seen from Section 2.3 that this allowance has been made within the current system.

2.2 THE PROJECT MANAGEMENT STRUCTURE

The project management structure is defined as those forms and procedures necessary to ensure adequate control of, and reporting on, the progress of each phase of a project.

This section is not concerned with the techniques of project management, but with the procedures by which information is recorded and progress monitored. There are, in fact, two types of information to be recorded:

(i)   That to be used in order to control the project and to make the subsequent analyses.
(ii) That to be used in order to control the operation of the company as a whole.

The latter of these two is not concerned with the management of a specific project, but rather the co-ordination of all the projects within the company. The current section is concerned only with the management control of projects and as such will only make reference to the interface with the company control and reporting structure and not describe the structure itself. The inputs required from the project manager by the company control and reporting structure will, of course, take some measure of her/his time. These inputs will be a requirement from management for information that will facilitate the financial control of the project and the forward planning of staff activities. The project manager will also gain

65

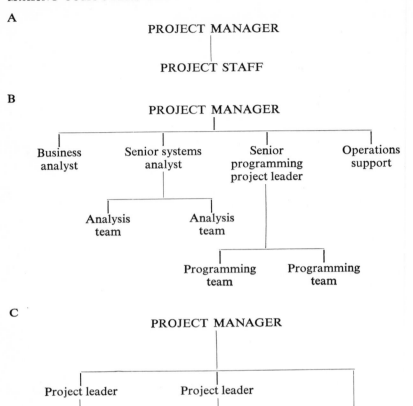

financial information from the company control and reporting structure that will enable him to keep the significance of the project to the overall company financial objective in perspective.

2.3 THE ELEMENTS OF THE PROJECT MANAGEMENT STRUCTURE

2.3.1 *Activities Prior to Each Phase of the Project*

Before any work can begin the scope of the current phase must be re-assessed and the appropriate check-lists completed and acted upon. The scope of the phase will then have been determined and the overall objectives clearly established.

It is not reasonable to expect the detailed estimates and schedules for

Project Management Structure Summary

Timescale	Activities	Documentation
Prior to the feasibility study	Recording all information gained in a clear, structured way	Appropriate sections of the PROJECT DEVELOPMENT FILE
Prior to each phase of the project	Estimating and scheduling activities. (Establishing timescales and resources required)	Record estimates and schedules in the appropriate parts of the: ACTIVITY CONTROL CHART PROGRESS AGAINST ESTIMATES PROJECT PROGRESS REPORT
	Requirements of the company management control and reporting structure	
DAILY	Recording and in some cases reviewing daily progress	Work record or time sheet ACTIVITY CONTROL CHART
	Becoming aware of and solving day-to-day problems	Notes for PROJECT PROGRESS REPORT
	Recording machine usage	Appropriate forms
WEEKLY	Recording, reviewing and reporting the week's progress.	ACTIVITY CONTROL CHART PROGRESS AGAINST ESTIMATES
	Setting targets for the following week	PROJECT PROGRESS REPORT
	Requirements of the company management control and reporting structure	
MONTHLY	Requirements of the company management control and reporting structure	
At end of each phase of the project	Review progress to date	Notes for use when writing the POST-PROJECT ANALYSIS
	Appraisals of staff leaving the project	STAFF APPRAISAL FORM
At final completion	Appraisals of staff leaving the project. Post-project analysis	STAFF APPRAISAL FORM POST-PROJECT ANALYSIS

NOTE: The appropriate sections of the PROJECT DEVELOPMENT FILE will be completed throughout the project.

all the phases of a project to be done at the very beginning; although an overall estimate of manpower, machine usage and costs will be required.

The detailed estimates and schedules will be prepared at the earliest point in time that all the necessary information is known. For example, for the system design phase this point in time will be when the feasibility study has been completed, and for program development when the program specifications have been completed.

Identifying activities and control points. The first stage in the production of estimates and schedules is to identify all of the activities that will be required in order to complete the current phase of the project. This exercise is done by the project manager and the project leaders concerned.

It is important to choose a level of activity that will facilitate a good measure of control. For example, to call the feasibility study an activity may, on a very small and simple project, be reasonable, whereas within a large complex project it will be required to be split into several activities. It is well to bear in mind that most activities will be subsequently divided into four or five sub-activities which will form the lowest level of control.

It is the project manager's responsibility to decide the scope of an activity, the sub-activities within that activity, and to ensure that these sub-activities are meaningful. Each sub-activity must comprise of a definite task or tasks which are self-contained and measurable.

Although a particular phase (e.g. the feasibility study) may be done by several people, an activity will not usually be assigned to more than two persons. This itself will put a constraint on the duration of an activity. It is difficult to make any points about the duration of an activity or sub-activity without setting a constraint on the project manager. However, some guidelines are given below which it is felt will generally apply, although the individual project manager can go outside these suggestions provided he/she is sure that adequate control will be applied.

Suggested effort and elapsed time for activities and control points

	Effort	Elapsed time
ACTIVITY	10–30 days	2–6 weeks
SUB-ACTIVITY	1–10 days	max. 2 weeks

Relating effort to elapsed time. Having identified all of the activities and sub-activities and determined the amount of effort that each one will take, this effort requirement must be related to an elapsed time to complete.

Prior to relating effort to elapsed time it is, of course, essential to know all of the holiday and training arrangements of the staff who will be working on the current phase of the project. It is also necessary to ensure that the people working on the project have the necessary skills appropriate to the activities they are to perform as it may be necessary to arrange for specialised training. If the above points are neglected, it could well seriously affect the project or the personal arrangements of the staff, both of which are equally important.

68

Similarly, there may be key events which either are not related to a specific activity or, more especially, fall outside the control of the project manager. An example of a key event is the first submission of input data by a user department. The dates associated with these key events are often crucial, and therefore must be carefully considered when relating effort to elapsed time. The progress of these key events must also be carefully monitored throughout the project.

There will always be constraints on either manpower, elapsed time or both. Clearly, if there are constraints on both, then one or the other must give way. The timescale is almost always the most important consideration so it is best to determine the manpower required to complete the current phase of the project within that timescale unless otherwise directed. The resulting manpower requirement can then be matched against available resources. Should the available resources fall short of those required, then the effect on the timescale must be determined and reported. The final result of this exercise will be a resource or resources allocated to each activity.

Estimating machine usage. This is an essential though not easy task. Compilations, tests and system testing runs will take varying times, depending on the machine used and the operating system by which the machine is controlled. Also, projects may well use more than one machine during the development of a system. It is sometimes more meaningful, when trying to assess performance, to know how many times a job has been submitted, for 10 submissions on a very fast machine may well use less time than 5 on a slower one. Once the total number of submissions have been determined for the current phase of the project, they will be multiplied by the average run-time for the particular type of work on the machine concerned. This figure will then be used as the estimate for the hours required on each machine.

Interface with other departments. It is very easy to overlook the delays that may be caused by not considering the way the project's workload will affect other departments. The best estimate must be made of the requirement for clerical staff, and this requirement made known to the appropriate supervisor in order that they can plan their workload. The machine usage estimates should be made known to the appropriate authority so that the workload can be scheduled. The importance of these simple steps cannot be overstressed.

Documenting the results of the estimating and scheduling. The effort required, machine usage and date for the completion of each sub-activity and activity will be recorded as described below.

ACTIVITY CONTROL CHART (see Appendix A, pages 73–74)
Fill in: PROJECT

PHASE
ACTIVITY
USER
SUB-ACTIVITY
with the appropriate information.
Complete the ESTIMATES TO COMPLETE section.

After completing the ACTIVITY CONTROL CHART, but before completing the relevant sections on the PROGRESS AGAINST ESTIMATES and PROJECT PROGRESS REPORT, the user (analyst, programmer, etc.) should be allowed to study the proposed schedule and make any comments. This exercise may result in some modification to the estimates and schedules.

PROGRESS AGAINST ESTIMATES (see Appendix B, pages 75–76)
Fill in: PROJECT
PHASE
ACTIVITY
USER
with the appropriate information.
Complete the ESTIMATES section.

PROJECT PROGRESS REPORT (see Appendix C, pages 77–78)
Partially prepare the PROJECT PROGRESS REPORTS for the current phase of the project
by completing: PROJECT
PHASE
PROJECT MANAGER
Also the following:
Within PROGRESS SUMMARY: KEY EVENTS
COMPLETION DATES/EST.
EFFORT/EST.
Within MACHINE USAGE: ESTIMATE
The PROJECT PROGRESS REPORT so completed can then be photocopied as many times as there are elapsed weeks to complete the phase of the project, plus a few more copies.

2.3.2 Daily Activities
The most important thing to be done daily is for the project leaders and project manager to keep in touch with the progress of the project in order to solve day-to-day problems before they get out of hand. Any member of staff who is falling behind on his/her schedule must be reviewed daily until there is certainty that no further slippage is occurring. In any event, all members of the project group working on an activity will be required to complete the appropriate part of the ACTIVITY CONTROL CHART.

70

2.3.3 *Weekly Activities*

These are the primary activities during which all of the information essential to effective control and management of a project is gathered.

On a small project, all of the necessary activities will be done by the project manager, but on larger projects the project leaders will be expected to review and comment upon the progress of their subordinate staff during the past week.

Reviewing the week's progress. This will be done by either the project leader or project manager, depending on the size of the project. Each member of staff will be interviewed in turn, and their progress against estimates over the previous week examined. Any reasons for delays or exceptional circumstances will be noted in the COMMENTS box on the ACTIVITY CONTROL CHART for future reference. The expected schedule for the next week's activities will then be determined and the c/f ESTIMATES TO COMPLETE inserted on the form. These will also be inserted as the b/f figures on the next week's form. The project member and project leader or manager will then complete the appropriate columns within the PROGRESS AGAINST ESTIMATES section on the PROGRESS AGAINST ESTIMATES form after having made any re-estimates necessary.

2.3.4 *Monthly Activities*

The primary period for project control and reporting is the week, and in terms of controlling a specific project, longer periods such as a month, quarter or year have a somewhat diminished significance. These periods are however very important as far as the company management control and reporting is concerned. There will therefore be a requirement monthly for the project manager to provide the necessary inputs to the company management and reporting structure.

2.3.5 *Activities at the End of Each Phase of the Project*

It is a necessary and sensible thing to review the overall progress of the project at the end of each phase. This task consists of the following activities:

(i)   Ensuring that all documentation on the phase just completed is up to date.

(ii) Clearing up all outstanding problems prior to the next phase being started.

(iii) Making notes on the phase just completed which will be used when writing the post-project analysis.

(iv) Looking back through the progress of each activity and noting any points which will help in producing more accurate estimates and control of subsequent phases.

(v)   Reading through the project file and ensuring that all requirements noted have been fulfilled.

(vi)   Make appraisals of all staff leaving the project.

The appraisals must be done as soon as possible in order to give the member of staff the fairest possible appraisal, as time will dull the memory, even though comments will have been recorded. It is also very important to ensure that a third party (normally the project leader) is present at the appraisal in order to minimise the possibility of any bias that may exist being written into the appraisal.

It is very easy to skimp on a review, but every effort must be made not to do this because any problem carried forward must eventually be solved and time only makes problems larger and more difficult to solve.

2.3.6   *Activities at Final Completion*
There are two main activities on final completion. These are:

The post-project analysis
Staff appraisals

It is very easy to take things easy once the pressures are off, or to forget the completed project and get involved in a new one. Therefore it is all too easy to forget the post-project analysis and, by doing so, fail to take full benefit of the lesson learned. The post-project analysis is the means by which new ideas and lessons learned can be passed on for the benefit of the company and the other project managers.

The post-project analysis takes the form of a basic text referencing an appendix which contains any papers or notes that can then be distributed for use as and when required. The analysis will take a differing form depending on what has to be said and the type of project concerned.

2.3.7   *Appendixes*

ICL Dataskil

APPENDIX A

Activity control chart

Project

Phase

Sub-activity

Contract No.

Loc. code

User

Activity

Comments

		Estimates to complete					Actual effort, machine usage								Totals	
		Effort (days)	Machine usage	Completion date		Week-ending date								Hours	Machine usage
						T	F	S	S	M	T	W			
b/f					Hours										
c/f					Machine										
b/f					Hours										
c/f					Machine										
b/f					Hours										
c/f					Machine										
b/f					Hours										
c/f					Machine										
b/f					Hours										
c/f					Machine										
b/f					Hours										
c/f					Machine										
b/f					Hours										
c/f					Machine										
b/f					Hours										
c/f					Machine										
Totals b/f					Hours										
c/f					Machine										

FORM 17/11 (8.73)

73

APPENDIX A

Instructions for completing the activity control chart

This form will be completed daily by all staff performing a defined activity within a project.

Project	The name by which the project is known, for example, *Brightwells Account System.*
Contract No.	The standard Dataskil contract number. This may be extended, if required, for particular local purposes, e.g. *W7741(R/1)*
Location code	The standard company location code.
Phase	A major sub-division of the project usually self-contained for example, *System Design or Program Development.*
Activity	The activity with which the form is concerned for example, *System Investigation Part 1 or Program BRO1.*
User	The person performing the activity.
Sub-activity	A suitable sub-division of the activity, for example, for activity *Program BRO1* two of the sub-activities could be, *Program Design* and *Flow-Charting.*
Estimates to complete	The B/F estimates are initially the original estimates. The C/F estimates are the re-estimates made weekly when reviewing progress. They become next weeks B/F estimates.
Effort (days)	The number of days required to complete the sub-activity or activity to the nearest ½ day.
Machine usage	In the case of sub-activities or activities requiring the use of a machine this is the estimated number of submissions or hours of machine time needed to complete the requirements of the sub-activity.
Completion date	The estimated completion date of the sub-activity or activity.
Actual (effort, machine usage)	
Week-ending date	The date of the Wednesday.
Hours	The hours spent on a particular sub-activity each day recorded to the nearest 6 minutes (0.1 hr), for example, 3.6.
Machine usage	The number of times a job was submitted for a run each day or the amount of time used.
Comments	Comments by the User, Project Leader or Project Manager on the progress of the sub-activity. The date completed will be shown when appropriate.
Totals	The totals for the *Estimates to complete (Effort days, machine and completion date)* and the weekly totals for *hours* and *machine usage* both for the activity and the sub-activities.

74

APPENDIX B

ICL Dataskil   Progress against estimates

Project		Contract No.		Loc. code		User	

Phase			Activity				

Estimates

Effort (days)		Machine usage			Completion date		

Progress against estimates

Week ending date	Effort				Machine usage				Completion date
	This week	To date	O/S	Variance	This week	To date	O/S	Variance	

Actual performance summary

Effort (days)		Machine usage			Completion date		

FORM 17/13 (8.73)

APPENDIX B

Instructions for completing the progress against estimates form

This form will be completed weekly by the Project Manager together with the Project Leader(s).

Project	The name by which the project is known, for example, *Brightwells Accounts System.*
Phase	A major sub-division of the project, usually self-contained, for example, *System Design or Program Development.*
Contract No.	The standard Dataskil contract number. This may be extended, if required, for particular local purposes, e.g. *W7741 (R/1)*
Location code	The standard company location code.
Activity	The activity with which the form is concerned, for example, *System Investigation Part 1 or Program BRO1.*
User	The person performing the activity.
Estimates	The original estimates for reference.
Effort (days)	The number of days required to complete the activity to the nearest ½ day.
Machine usage	In the case of activities requiring the use of a machine this is the estimated number of submissions or hours of machine time needed to complete the requirements of the activity.
Completion date	The estimated completion date of the activity.
Progress against estimates	
Week ending date	The date of the Wednesday.
Effort (machine usage)	The effort and machine usage *this week, to date* and *O/S* (outstanding). *Variance* is calculated by taking the difference between the *ITo date + O/S* figures and the appropriate estimates; + indicating better and - indicating worse.
Completion date	The latest estimated completion date and finally the actual completion date.
Actual performance summary	The actual *effort (days), machine usage,* and *date completed* shown as a positive or negative variance against the estimate.

76

APPENDIX C

ICL Dataskil   Project progress report

Project		Contract No.	Loc. code	W.E. date
Phase		Project manager		

Progress summary

Key events	Completion dates		
	Estimate	Last week	This week

Effort

Estimate	This week	To date	O/S

Effort variance

Last week	This week

Machine usage

Machine	Estimate	This week	To date	Needed
Totals				

Exception report   Action

FORM 17/12 (8.73)

APPENDIX C

Instructions for completing the project progress report

This form will be completed weekly by the Project Manager.

Project
The name by which the project is known for example, *Brightwells Accounts System.*

Contract No.
The standard Dataskil contract number. This may be extended, if required, for particular local purposes, e.g. *W7741 (R/1)*

Location code
The standard company location code.

Week-ending date
The date of the Wednesday.

Phase
A major sub-division of the project usually self-contained, for example, *System Design* or *Program Development.*

Project Manager
The name of the Project Manager.

Progress summary
This is a summary of all the activities within the phase concerned.

Key events
Events significant to the progress of the project, for example, completion of the design of a sub-suite or, vital data due from a user department.

Completion dates
The original *estimate, last week* and *this week* dates.

Effort
The original *estimate, this week, to date* and O/S (outstanding) figures.

Effort variance
The *Effort Variance this week* is calculated by taking *Effort to Date + Effort O/S — Effort estimated;* + against the variance indicates better and — worse than estimated.

Machine usage

Machine
The machine used, for example *Putney 1902S.*

Estimate
The estimated amount of machine time to be used.

This week
The actual machine time used this week.

To date
The machine time used to date.

Needed
The estimated number of hours still needed on the particular machine.

Exception report
Brief notes on all events and exceptional circumstances. If a full report is required it will be referenced and attached.

Action
The action taken in response to the events and exceptional circumstances notes in the exception report. This may also be a reference to more full notes which will be attached or the name(s) of the person(s) required to take the action.

78

Chapter 4

The Selection and Justification of Projects

The Need for Project Selection Procedures

The data processing department is, as we have seen, a support unit intended to help the major line departments in achieving their objectives. When we examine an organisation as a whole, or look into the structure of a particular division, it is possible to identify several opportunities to deploy the resources of the data processing department. It is, however, possible to take advantage of only some of these opportunities, and so it is important to select them carefully. In this chapter a method for controlling the selection process is proposed, and this method is fundamentally aimed at the justification of new projects for an organisation already using a computer. It could apply equally to the purchase of a computer.

In some organisations, the data processing manager is left very much alone to make decisions on the relative importance of projects, and invariably he gets a reputation for being inflexible and unhelpful in responding to requests for new systems or system changes. He should be trying to give an equal level of service to all the people who require his help, but is usually constrained by his level of manpower and the hardware available from carrying out new work. Alternatively, if he doesn't protect his resources from being overcommitted, he may earn the reputation of never being able to make and keep effectively to the schedules. Thus he badly needs a methodology for determining the importance of new systems required within the organisation, and he needs a forum in which the managers, who are his main users, can meet to discuss the merits and urgency of new assignments objectively.

Every new system proposed should be evaluated to ascertain its potential contribution to the profitability or efficiency of the organisation. This contribution should be assessed after taking into account the likely development and operational costs of the system proposed. It is also important for the senior management to be deeply involved in this process so that their judgement and experience can be used in assessing factors relating to the everyday business of the organisation.

Characteristically, informal lobbying takes place to promote particular projects; and although this approach creates an atmosphere of competition which may induce the protagonists to divine real cost/benefits, it is a very haphazard method. It sometimes causes worthwhile projects to be suppressed while those people who are politically active, or who have large budgets to manipulate, achieve recognition for projects which have less potential than others going forward. Ideally, therefore, it is desirable to have a standard approach to the evaluation of investment in different projects.

In every case, the decisions should be made by the policy making management with the advice of the technical specialists, who are going to develop the system, and the line management, who are going to implement and run it.

In Chapter 2, we called the policy making group the *systems management committee* and the term *project management* was used to represent the line and data processing management team responsible for a project. The precise structure of these groups and the level at which they are established will vary from one organisation to another, but, as a guideline, let us say that the systems management committee consists of executive directors and other professional executives such as the chief accountant; and it will, of course, include the management services manager.

The importance of having a high-level body to evaluate and approve projects regularly is that it can develop a standard approach to the problem and have the benefit of considering each proposal against others which are current. It can also make sure that approved projects are in accord with general policies and overall business plans.

This arrangement is adopted by most organisations for monitoring any investment which requires a high level of capital expenditure, but it is not often utilised with computer projects which do not require the authorisation of new hardware. Thus it is not uncommon to see thousands of pounds of man effort expended without the board being fully aware and in control.

Of course, it is essential not to inundate the senior management who serve on the systems management committee with minor requests for systems. Therefore it is advisable to have some expenditure ceiling below which senior management approval is not required. If this figure is set too high, it will follow that many short-term and ad hoc assignments may be initiated by line managers to escape the rigours of the selection procedure. It is important to allow for the selection and control of both long-term and short-term investment projects, and to balance the allocation of development resources in these directions.

It is possible for the senior management to set up a subsidiary committee to deal with less important investments, and perhaps to arrange the project funding procedure so that minor investment requests are financed by the originating departments. Even so, senior management must be concerned to see that resources are not diverted from the major investments that they have approved.

The Requirements of the Selection Procedure

The selection process should include a quantitive evaluation of each project established jointly by the data processing staff and the line management. The evaluation should provide a focus for answers to the following questions:

(a) Why is this project important?
(b) What are the effects if the system is not implemented?
(c) How much will it cost to develop?
(d) How much will the system cost to run?
(e) What improvements will it make in the business?
(f) When can those improvements be obtained?
(g) When will additional investment be necessary to sustain the improvements?

In a straightforward situation, the line managers should be able to forecast the economic improvements that they expect from a new system. The data processing staff should be able to say whether these improvements are feasible, and at what cost. The improvements should be capable of being expressed as a reduction in expenditure and/or an increase in revenue, and thus a graph such as that shown in Figure 4.1 can be drawn. This diagram illustrates how the costs start from the moment the decision is taken to carry out an initial investigation.

If this investigation indicates that there are benefits in continuing with the project, the development expenditure is approved and detailed design work and programming take place. Provided the benefits of the system remain worthwhile when re-examined at each appropriate milestone, the project will continue through to implementation until parallel running is completed and the system goes live. The system will probably not go live at one time; it is likely that benefits will be obtained progressively as parts of the new system begin to take effect. Eventually the system will reach full operational efficiency and will have then completely replaced the previous system. Thereafter the system should produce a continuing return each month until it, in turn, is replaced.

The following points have been marked on the graph in Figure 4.1:

$$A = \text{The project start}$$
$$B = \text{Maximum net investment}$$
$$C = \text{The break-even point}$$
$$D = \text{Planned cumulative return}$$

These four points provide parameters around which a policy can be formulated for selecting worthwhile projects. The precise details of the policy will differ from one organisation to another, since different managements will have individual views about what constitutes a good investment. However, let us attempt to provide some reasonable standards to illustrate the approach.

81

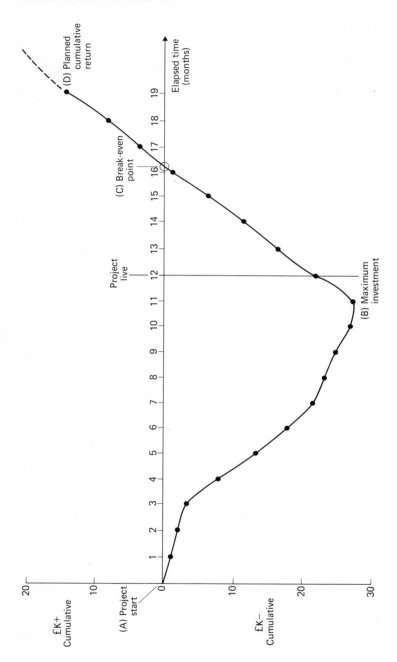

Figure 4.1 *Cumulative costs/benefits of a project.*

(a) The break-even point must occur within thirty months of the project start;
      and
(b) the break-even point must occur within eighteen months of the system going live;
      and
(c) the planned cumulative return must be greater than maximum net investment after thirty-six months from project start.

Guidelines such as these provide an overall standard within which all projects can be examined by the systems management committee. The line management will be obliged to seek projects which produce a desired level of return, and the data processing staff will be encouraged to think of their services as part of the company's investment in the future.

Of course, some degree of monitoring must take place regularly to ensure that line managers do not make frivolous and over-optimistic claims for their favourite projects. This monitoring can take place when reviewing projects against milestones, and in post-implementation audits. Projects which fail to live up to the standard required should be scrapped as soon as the condition is diagnosed.

Analysing Cost/Benefits
It is not necessary to go into a complicated analysis to be able to draw graphs of the kind shown in Figure 4.1. Neither is it necessary to use the graph itself as a means of displaying cost/benefits. It is helpful, however, in comparing one project against another to present information in a standard manner.

I think it is important also to use a method which can be understood by a wide range of people in the organisation. For this reason, I do not recommend, except for very large corporate projects, the use of techniques such as *discounted cash flow*. This would tend to make the analysis somewhat of a specialised operation, and introduce complexities and problems which are not always strictly relevant. Financial analysts and corporate planners are expensive people to deploy in evaluating the average data processing project, and this type of analysis, apart from any arguments concerning the applicability on technical grounds, is not warranted except in major corporate exercises.

Figure 4.2 shows a very simple analysis of the return from a typical data processing project. It is broken into three parts. First of all, the various factors which contribute to the development costs are listed and the expenditure is phased over the development period, in this case twelve months. Then the running costs of the system per month and the proposed benefits are listed. Finally, the cumulative costs and benefits are netted off to show the return from the project over the first eight months of the live running period.

Superficially, the project illustrated in Figure 4.2 appears to be a good

83

PROJECT TITLE SALES LEDGER AND DEBTOR ENQUIRY SYSTEM

PROPOSAL ISSUE NO. 1 **DATE** 17.4.74

DESCRIPTION To maintain sales ledger from current invoicing system, and allocate cash and provide exception reporting for debtor control

SUMMARY

PROJECT LIVE (MONTHS)	14
BREAK-EVEN POINT (MONTHS)	27
CUMULATIVE BENEFIT 36 MONTHS (£K)	48.7
CUMULATIVE BENEFIT 48 MONTHS (£K)	104.7
MAXIMUM NETT INVESTMENT (£K)	41.1

EXPENDITURE (£K)	1st Year				2nd Year				3rd Year				4th Year			
	1	2	3	4	1	2	3	4	1	2	3	4	1	2	3	4
1. DEVELOPMENT COSTS (£K)																
1.1 Systems & programming	3.0	13.4	5.3	1.0												
1.2 Machine time		0.6	0.7	1.0												
1.3 Other (Specify overleaf)		0.4	0.6	1.2												
2. RUNNING COSTS (£K)																
2.1 Data preparation					1.2	1.2	1.4	1.4	1.6	1.6	1.6	1.6	2.0	2.0	2.0	2.0
2.2 Machine time					9.6	9.6	10.0	10.0	11.0	11.0	11.0	11.0	12.0	12.0	12.0	12.0
2.3 Clerical effort				3.0	2.5	2.5	2.5	2.5	2.5	2.5	2.5	2.5	3.0	3.0	3.0	3.0
2.4 Program maintenance																
2.5 Other (Specify overleaf)					0.6	0.6	0.6	0.6	0.6	0.6	0.6	0.6	1.0	1.0	1.0	1.0
3. TOTAL EXPENDITURE (£K)	3.0	14.4	6.6	6.2	13.9	13.9	14.5	14.5	15.7	15.7	15.7	15.7	18.0	18.0	18.0	18.0
4. CUMULATIVE EXPENDITURE (£K)	3.0	17.4	24.0	30.2	44.1	58.0	72.5	87.0	102.7	118.4	134.1	149.8	167.8	185.8	203.8	221.8
5. TOTAL BENEFITS (Specify overleaf)	–	–	–	–	3.0	14.5	30.0	30.0	30.0	30.0	30.0	30.0	32.0	32.0	32.0	32.0
6. CUMULATIVE BENEFITS (£K)	–	–	–	–	3.0	17.5	47.5	77.5	107.5	137.5	167.5	197.5	229.5	261.5	293.5	325.5
7. CASH FLOW (£K)	(3.0)	(14.4)	(6.6)	(6.2)	(10.9)	1.6	15.5	15.5	14.3	14.3	14.3	14.3	14.0	14.0	14.0	14.0
8. CUMULATIVE CASH FLOW (£K)	(3.0)	(17.4)	(24.0)	(30.2)	(41.1)	(39.5)	(24.0)	(8.5)	5.8	20.1	34.4	48.7	62.7	76.7	90.7	104.7

AUTHORISATION

LINE MANAGEMENT	MANAGEMENT SERVICES	SYSTEMS MANAGEMENT COMMITTEE
H.V. Williams	K.R. Hoare	N.V.K K.L.K

FORM DP11 – FINANCIAL EVALUATION

COST/BENEFIT CHECK LIST

1. Development expenses ⎫
2. Running expenses   ⎬ Delete any two
3. Benefits   ⎭

Sheet ☐ of ☐

Month (month 1 = project start)

Item											
1 Systems and Programming											
2 Machine time											
3 Data preparation											
4 Other labour											
5 Accommodation											
6 Equipment rental											
7 Equipment depreciation											
8 Equipment maintenance											
9 Telecommunications											
10 Interest charges											
11 Transport											
12 DP materials											
13 Other materials											
14 Insurance											
15 Stationery											
16 Training											
17											
18											
19											
20											
21											
22											
23											
24											
25											

FORM DP 12

Figure 4.3 Cost/benefit check list.

project. It certainly fulfils the criteria we listed in the preceding pages as minimum standards for approval of a project. However, we cannot let this analysis stand without some probing and checking of the factors used in the analysis.

In reviewing the project, the systems management committee must seek to satisfy themselves that the line management and data processing staff have carefully and objectively assessed the costs and benefits. An important question also, but one we will not discuss here, is whether the senior management consider that the people involved are capable of realising the opportunities offered.

Bearing in mind the difficulties in estimating the cost and duration of computer development projects which we identified in Chapter 2, some reservations will be entertained concerning the schedule of costs. The following questions will serve to put this side of the argument under sharper focus:

(a) Does this project equate with any previous one in complexity or size?
(b) How do the estimates compare with those made in similar situations previously, and what was the actual performance in those cases?
(c) Are any new techniques or hardware and software innovations being introduced?
(d) Do other organisations have experience of these new techniques and what problems have they encountered?
(e) Does the data processing department have the necessary resources to take on this extra project?
(f) What other projects will suffer if this one is implemented or if it absorbs more resources than planned?
(g) Do the data processing people believe that the proposed system will produce the benefits claimed by the line manager?

If there are any doubts on these issues, the reviewing managers can seek a further study and a report at an early date. By so doing, they will make it clear that they expect objective and firm advice.

The systems management committee must seek with due vigour to expose any flaws which may exist in the line management's advocacy in favour of the system, and to form a judgement about the importance and probability of achieving the benefits claimed. The following questions will assist in an evaluation:

(a) Do the line management see the project as being vital to achieving their objectives?
(b) Are they prepared to quantify the improvements that this will make in their operations?
(c) Are these improvements sufficiently tangible and large enough in volume to be worthwhile even if costs of the new system are larger than expected?

(d) If the new system reduces operational costs in departments, are the users prepared to give up a proportion of their budget accordingly, upon implementation?

(e) Have other organisations successfully implemented systems of a similar nature, and what has been their experience?

(f) If there is a high degree of risk in the project, ask the most experienced managers in the organisation for their opinion of the project.

The Nature of Benefits

It is usual to find that opportunities for major benefits exist in the principal operating units of the organisation, i.e. where labour and materials are extensively used. This may be, for example, in production planning and control systems, in inventory control, or in major commercial procedures. It is in these situations that benefits will be easily demonstrated.

Other important areas will be at points in the organisation where control can be exerted over the flow of cash into and out of the company, e.g. the sales ledger or purchasing operations. Improvements in the speed with which information is collated and transmitted will enable operational units to control debtors and inventory levels, and to obtain supplies at bulk discounts. These benefits may be less easy to quantify, but the line managers responsible should be urged to do so and their achievements should be monitored.

Even less easily quantified are the benefits resulting from a general improvement in management information. Yet many systems are implemented simply to provide managers with information. I would question the usefulness and validity of much of the output produced by such systems, and suggest that the managers receiving the information should be pressed to justify the way in which it will enable them to improve their operations. Sometimes it will be found that the information is a vital part of the control that must exist, but too often such systems are continued long after the original need has been satisfied.

Personnel information systems are an example of the kind of information system which may be difficult to justify. It is necessary to produce the payroll, and certain statutory returns about staff may have to be generated. In addition, management may believe it important to keep certain historical data to assist in discussions with union representatives. Statistical information to assist in manpower planning may require to be generated. However, the cost of maintaining individual data elements on the personnel file should be considered, and any items which do not earn their keep should be excluded.

It is also worth considering whether the data can be accurately maintained. Data elements which do not get updated by primary procedures cannot be maintained with accuracy and so the information generated will be useless.

When a manager of a user department insists on a particular report from a system, he should be obliged to justify his need. Most times the answer is, 'I cannot do my job properly without it.' This implies one of two things:

(a) He can quantify an improvement that he is seeking in his present performance.
(b) Due to a change in the business, his job objectives are altered and a new system is required.

Whatever the case, steps should be taken to answer the questions:

(a) Is a computer system necessary, or can a local system bring about the desired improvement?
(b) Is the manager responsible prepared to forecast what the improvements in performance will be in financial terms?
(c) Is the manager concerned prepared to meet the operational costs of the system in his budget?

The benefits claimed by managers generally fall into two categories:

(a) Tangible benefits.
(b) Intangible benefits.

The tangible benefits are those more easily quantified. The intangible benefits are usually claims submitted for tangible ones by managers who are not prepared to commit themselves.

In any operation which provides a service to line organisations, claims for intangible benefits tend to be encountered too frequently. In a warehousing operation, for example, the distribution manager may claim that, using his present resources, he can improve the volume of products which he can ship to retail outlets. Here the manager is not prepared to forgo any of his current resources, but claims to be able to increase his output. This benefit has really to be assessed by those receiving his output, and they must participate by forecasting the improvements in revenue which will result.

Similar situations arise in financial accounting departments. The outputs from the systems used by such a department are used to produce statutory accounts and protect the assets of the organisation, but also to provide information to management for control purposes. The need to improve the volumes of information handled, or the accuracy and speed with which it is generated should be capable of translation into tangible benefits.

The most difficult benefits to justify are those which are claimed to impart an improvement in management control. If a divisional manager insists on certain information being available in order to help him meet his financial objectives, he should be prepared to include in his budget the costs for the development and operation of the system. The whole question of how projects are funded is an interesting and important area, and a full discussion appears in Chapter 5.

Improvements in service to customers are also difficult to assess. Usually these are an attempt to protect or increase the existing customer base: in effect, an attempt to improve the level of revenue. For example, many large international airlines have invested in reservations systems to improve their service to travellers and booking agents. In the times when airlines were heavily overloaded, this enabled the more advanced companies to expand at the expense of those which were not able to impart so good a service to their customers. These investments were massive, and probably out of proportion to any economic advantages obtained. Today, many of the smaller airlines are trying to follow suit when it is probably in their more immediate interests to concentrate on improving control over their ground operations. There must be a considerable degree of risk attached to dedicated projects of the 'reservations' type, but the management may feel satisfied that they cannot achieve their planned growth without it. A much more sophisticated form of project evaluation is desirable in such cases, and the feasibility should be established only with the participation of the full resources of the corporate planning department. Organisations not having strength in this area would be advised to seek the aid of consultants.

Finally, many projects may be justified by the improvements in the efficiency of the data processing departments themselves. A significant reduction in the amount of computer time required to run a particular system may enable some items of data processing equipment to be returned to the manufacturer or to be used for other important projects, thus deferring the need to purchase or rent other equipment at some future date. Since most existing systems will be less than optimally efficient, the data processing department may be able to include benefits of this nature, along with those claimed by the user departments, whenever a system is considered for amendment. However, it is important to justify the existence of the system in the first place, since the overall benefits to the organisation may be greater if the system is abandoned altogether.

This kind of objectivity can be encouraged by the way in which the systems management committee goes about its task. If the general attitude of management is healthily inclined towards setting and meeting performance targets, the probability is that it will create an environment in which the people in management services functions can greatly contribute to the achievement of corporate objectives. The computer can be made to pay its way and to encourage managers to seek levels of performance which are not possible by other means.

SUMMARY OF CHAPTER 4

1   The selection of applications is the most crucial aspect of computing, so this function and the determination of priorities should not be left to the data processing management.

89

2 A methodology for selecting applications is required, and a forum must be established with senior management in which the merits and priorities of new applications can be discussed.

3 Every new system should be evaluated to ascertain its potential contribution to the profitability, or efficiency, of the organisation.

4 The selection procedure should include a quantitive evaluation of each project.

5 The benefits claimed for any new system must be supported by the line managers who are going to be responsible for the system concerned.

6 The estimate of costs must be made by, or accepted by, the data processing management.

7 The line managers and the data processing management must be responsible for achieving the planned cost/benefits if the project receives top management approval.

8 Projects which appear to have marginal benefits only should be abandoned, since development or operational costs could well rise to offset the benefits.

9 The benefits should be reviewed at a number of planned milestones in project development.

10 A standard method of financial evaluation should be adopted to ensure that all projects are assessed in the same manner.

11 An organisation should establish common parameters to govern the selection of data processing projects, which are consistent with other types of investment that the company may undertake.

12 Audits should be conducted to monitor whether benefits are achieved in practice, and line managers must be compelled to justify their subsequent performance using the new system.

Chapter 5

Funding Information Systems

Budgeting for Projects

Senior management is frequently perplexed by the problem of establishing the level of financial resources to devote to data processing activity.

Since data processing services are used throughout an organisation to support the various divisions and departments that may exist, it follows that the process of creating budgets is difficult and requires multilateral communication. Perhaps the most common method, once the data processing department has established itself with a few major projects, is to allow the expenditure budget to be incremented by inflationary movements as each year goes by. Ten per cent per annum may be the norm until the company meets a difficult trading period, whereupon the axe will be wielded arbitrarily and the data processing budget will be among the first to receive treatment. This is not an objective way to establish the level of activity of such an important department.

One way of resolving the problem is to charge the full costs of the service to the various user departments. The costs of both development work and of live running systems can be handled in this way in the hope that economic forces affecting the various divisions and departments will result in a rational level of demand for data processing activity. The arguments in favour of this approach include:

(a)   The users will be encouraged to seek the most profitable ways of deploying the data processing resources.
(b)   The annual budget will emerge more or less automatically as an aggregate of the different negotiations between the management services manager and the senior executives in user departments. Users will have to plan their use of the data processing resources and build appropriate allocations into their budgets.
(c)   The users will be encouraged to avoid unnecessary delays to projects since they are having to meet the costs of analysts and programmers assigned to their projects.

There are, however, disadvantages if this approach is followed in isolation. Some of these problems have been identified in the preceding chapter when we discussed project selection and control. The main disadvantage lies in the tendency for users to become excessively parochial in their attitudes, because the approach provides a strong barrier to the development of systems which span organisational units. It encourages users to duplicate files and information systems which are not mutually coherent. A mass of data may be processed and good local systems may emerge, but the overall effect can be to present senior management with inconsistent and irreconcilable facts.

Corporate Development Budget
In discussing the systems management committee in Chapter 3, we stressed the need for project selection procedures which enable corporate objectives to be recognised. We implied the need for sanctions to be exercised on projects, and it follows from this that a development budget should be controlled by the systems management committee. The procedure can be arranged so that systems which are going to have major benefits across the organisation, and systems which are aimed significantly to improve particular problem areas in the company, are funded from the development budget and are developed under the critical eye of the systems management committee.

New developments which are solely for the use of particular departments, and have very little corporate significance, should still be brought before the systems management committee for approval. The approval for implementation should be given provided the data processing manager does not consider that such projects will prevent him from achieving some other more significant aims; and provided that each project concerned satisfies the basic cost/benefit standards established, and that the user is prepared to meet development costs.

Thus development work can be regarded in two categories :

(a) That which has major corporate benefits and can be supported by the corporate development budget.
(b) That which has benefits to only a specific department and requires the department to meet development costs.

This arrangement can encourage users to aim for overall corporate benefits and may help to favour the selection of projects which have long-term rather than short-time advantages. It may also allow departments to go for benefits on a larger scale than would be the case if they were left to their own devices.

Maintenance and Ad Hoc Projects
Another irritating thing about computer projects is that they never seem to end – someone is always tinkering about amending files or getting out a

new report for management. I suppose it must be a good sign if a systems department recognises that systems need to adapt to the real world in which they operate. However, these activities can be very costly and absorb resources which may be better deployed elsewhere.

The charge-back mechanism should be used to encourage user departments to rationalise their requests for this type of development work. The data processing manager will be able to plan his resources more effectively if users are prepared to signify their need for ad hoc information by paying for it.

Charging for Operational Systems

When systems become operational, the user departments should bear *all* the operational costs; and if several departments use the same system, the costs can be shared accordingly.

Another problem concerns the support which different user departments have to provide in making a system viable. For example, the collection, preparation, validation and correction of basic data may be the responsibility of a prime user department. If the system is used widely by many other departments, the prime user department may have to control the data in accordance with standards which are not strictly relevant to its own operation. Unless this is recognised by the inclusion of an appropriate amount in the expenditure budget, the prime user will not be inclined to give the task the emphasis it deserves and, inevitably, the quality and usefulness of the system will suffer.

Figure 5.1 depicts a situation in which a major database is shared by several users. Here it is arranged that a prime user is responsible for the data collection and control, the management services department are allocated funds to control the main file maintenance procedures, and individual user departments are charged for the operation of their particular sub-systems.

All output from the system should be charged to the users, and they should also bear the costs of all terminal equipment to which they have exclusive use, and also a proportion of any computer equipment which drives those terminals. The purpose of charging costs back to the users is solely to encourage them to consider the economics of the system and its importance to them in running their particular operation. The actual mechanism for charging need not be complex, and it is not always justified to arrange complex accounting systems for this purpose. The factors that need to be considered in recovering the costs of systems run on behalf of user departments include:

(a)   Computer processing time.
(b)   Storage media used and retained for security.
(c)   Stationery.
(d)   Data control and job control manpower.
(e)   Copying, binding and distribution of output.
(f)   Data preparation.

93

Some of these costs may fluctuate each time the job is run, whereas some will be relatively constant throughout the life of the job. There is a case, particularly for routine batch processing, to consider making a fixed charge for a given job, or a charge based upon the number of transactions handled. The charge can be reviewed periodically, or even be adjusted

Figure 5.1 *The allocation of operational costs for a database.*

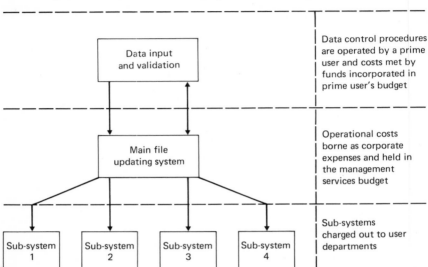

seasonally to reflect more closely actual resource utilisation. This can avoid the necessity for having to account for all the individual activities entailed in running the job on each occasion. However, since it is important for the data processing manager to measure and record the utilisation of these resources, it may not be a hardship to produce detailed job accounts as a by-product.

Much of the accounting information required for analysing the computer's utilisation can be obtained from the computer log – a record kept by the operating system of the computer which can be analysed by a program. Such an accounting system is essential in on-line situations where a user's utilisation of the central computing resource fluctuates according to the use made of his terminal in a given period.

Operational costs of live systems should be reviewed routinely. The system may not be efficient or effective even though the user is prepared to justify it by budgeting to meet the costs. A regular audit of an organisations systems will usually reveal many weaknesses. Not only can material benefits be identified in user departments, but hardware utilisation can be monitored and rationalised, thus avoiding the acquisition of new hardware simply to offset poor procedure design in the first place. Resultant recommendations to the systems management committee can thus identify potential benefits for further development. A separate section is devoted to the systems audit function (see Chapter 9, page 132).

The Data Processing Department as a Separate Company

Some large multidivisional organisations have established their computing department as a service company to provide the services of software and systems development to the various divisions, and to operate as a computer bureau to run the production systems as a routine service. This is really the extreme example of the use of a charge-back mechanism.

The advantages include many of those quoted earlier, but this arrangement also has attractions in resolving the problem endemic in multidivisional companies, i.e. the tendency to duplicate hardware and skilled manpower resources. The ownership, control and development of data processing is then effectively in one set of hands, and better resource utilisation should result. Skills can also be redeployed more readily to different parts of the corporation according to the needs prevailing.

There is also a less reasonable argument: that the opportunity to manage the service company gives important experience to young executives. Proponents of the service company concept also argue that surplus capacity within the company can be directed to earning revenue from agencies external to the organisation. This is one of the big traps in the concept.

The important thing is to be objective – the service company exists to support the other divisions in the group. The attractions of earning external revenue may lead to confused objectives which may affect the service given to other divisions. I have seen loss-making service companies, competing with software houses for external contracts, place other contracts externally while operating divisions within their own organisation, or set up their own units internally in competition with the service company.

To avoid this situation, some control has to be exercised by the parent organisation, which, in the long run, ends up having to spend time in formulating policies which it had hoped to avoid when setting up the service company originally.

Of course, many such companies have been successful, particularly at some key phase in the development of a computing policy within the group. Much depends on the personality of the man who leads the service company. For the policy to work, the manager of the service company will need a monopoly within the group, and he will constantly need to convince the various divisional heads that the service which his organisation provides is efficient and effective.

On balance, I am not in favour of the service company idea. It creates a sense of difference between the systems designers and their customers and inhibits the essential cross-fertilisation which should take place. It also has a tendency to work against the possibility of developing systems with group-wide benefits, leading instead to self-sufficient systems within parochial boundaries.

SUMMARY OF CHAPTER 5

1   To resolve the problems of closely managing the data processing resources, the top management of organisations often use charge-back mechanisms to force a rationalisation of the utilisation of these resources.
2   This approach encourages users to seek the most profitable ways of deploying computing power.
3   Also it encourages managers to plan their expenditure on data processing.
4   The main disadvantage is that it may encourage the development of parochial attitudes in implementing systems.
5   It also has a tendency to allow information systems to provide results which are not mutually coherent when considering the group as a whole.
6   A corporate development budget administered by the systems management committee is recommended to encourage developments which benefit the group.
7   Systems of local significance should be developed at the cost of the local departments, unless substantial benefits are attainable and require a level of investment exceeding the final resources of the local department.
8   Maintenance and ad hoc work should be funded by local departments to encourage them to rationalise their requests.
9   All routine production work should be charged to the user departments.
10   All production systems should be audited annually.
11   The use of computer service companies within multidivisional companies is a method of rationalising the ownership and deployment of data processing resources within the group.
12   The service company concept is only valid if it is operated objectively to provide an efficient and effective service to using divisions.

Chapter 6

Evaluating a Management Information System (MIS)

WHY HAVE MANAGEMENT INFORMATION SYSTEMS?

The term *management information system* was probably coined soon after the introduction of commercial computers, and much has been written about such systems since that date. Many managements were sold on the idea that an MIS would make them much more powerful and efficient as an organisation, and by the mid 1960s many companies had embarked on ambitious schemes. By 1970, there were many casualties and very few companies had got anywhere near achieving their original aims. It is probable that many had not been able clearly to define their aims.

It is very difficult to define a management information system, even within a particular organisation. It is an entity which must be continually changing to represent the current state of the organisation and its real-world environment. Given that it is extremely difficult to define what an MIS should consist of, it is perhaps surprising that so many organisations were prepared to spend so much money in pursuing the concept.

There have, however, been some notable success stories, the exact number perhaps depending on how big and all-embracing one considers such a system must be before it qualifies to bear the MIS label. Some organisations have attempted the total management information system approach, which is intended to integrate all the company's primary procedures and information flows. Others have sought to limit their ambitions to particular divisions of the organisation, or to certain kinds of data only.

I have said in Chapter 4 on project selection that it pays to be very hard-nosed about computer projects, and that assignments which do not seem likely to produce real economic benefits in a reasonably short period of time should be abandoned. I believe this to be fundamentally the right attitude. Since it is also very difficult to predict the benefits of a management information system, it follows that I would not encourage too many organisations to go for an MIS approach. However, there are some other factors to be considered.

97

First, many organisations could achieve real benefits from an MIS system simply by facing up to the data control requirements when data is integrated into mutually coherent file systems. For example, a company that earnt its revenue by renting and maintaining capital equipment was able to uncover a substantial degree of lost revenue when it integrated three previously independent files concerned with invoicing, asset control and maintenance.

Secondly, an MIS implies that data is organised in such a way that both routine and ad hoc information can be generated at short notice in response to situations which suddenly confront managers. It is very difficult to put a value on this except by experience in use of the system. In practice, the most important decisions facing managers are often in response to non-routine situations. The value of a system which supports management in this way can be established only by experience.

Finally, most senior executives and directors find themselves frustrated by the contradictory and incompatible statistics which emerge from independent file systems. Any system which is set up to serve a particular operational requirement is invariably in conflict with results produced by other systems which may use some data elements in common. This factor alone can provide a powerful motive for establishing a consistent and reliable management information system.

These considerations lead to some preliminary definitions of qualities required in management information systems:

Relevance of information: Data must be accurate, relevant and up to date, and reflect current events within the company and its real world environment.
Coherence of information: Data must be mutually coherent so that consistent and compatible information can be generated.
Response required by management: Managers must have ready access to the information which may have to be assembled quickly in response to non-routine situations.

RELEVANCE OF INFORMATION

The first of these qualities needs careful consideration when determining the scope of any proposed management information system. Real-time information systems, i.e. systems which can provide an up-to-the-minute picture of what is happening in an organisation, will be very complex and expensive to implement. A real-time management information system is almost certainly not a realistic objective for any organisation, except in some specific dedicated application which constitutes a major part of the organisation's business. Usually real-time systems are justified by the benefits that they bring to major operational divisions within an organisation, ·e.g. reservations systems used by airlines or tour operators.

When talking about an up-to-date management information system we

98

are not necessarily concerned with real-time, nor an on-line, means of access. We are concerned more with the frequency with which the files are updated in relation to the use which managers may wish to make of them. Most of the routine decisions and controlling actions taken by managers can be based upon highly summarised information provided routinely on either a daily, weekly, monthly or quarterly basis. Obviously the closer the involvement of an individual with operational responsibilities, the more frequently will he require information. Thus, in a warehousing operation, the following requirements may be evident:

(a) The operatives in the order department may need up-to-the-minute information about stocks to allocate against orders, and perhaps require to progress individual customer demands.
(b) The purchasing manager will need daily exception reports of critical stock situations as well as routine weekly and monthly reports to assist in management of the inventory.
(c) The chief accountant may require monthly reports to assist in the preparation of routine financial statements.
(d) Since so much management activity is concerned with responding to non-routine problems, all levels of management may wish now and then for *ad hoc* reports showing a particular situation which has not been previously reported upon.
(e) Those managers and staff concerned with strategic issues may also require to use models to operate upon summarised historical data to ask questions of the type, 'What happens if . . . ?'

The information is only relevant to an individual if the content is appropriate to his function, and if it is accurate and received in sufficient time to enable controlling action to be taken. The database from which the information is drawn must be updated to reflect the current and potential needs of its users, and the structure of the database must allow for changing requirements and priorities. There must clearly be an overall plan for its development which is consistent and supported by the management throughout the organisation.

In essence, such a plan would have to entail the intention to harness progressively all the major streams of data within the organisation. The database must be built up from the grass-roots procedures of the company by capturing and processing all the basic transactions which form part of the company's primary business operations. These transactions can then be reconciled one with another and organised routinely into a file system which can be used to drive the company's systems as well as providing for the needs of management for non-routine information.

This ideal is illustrated in Figure 6.1. In practice, there are few technical limitations in achieving such a scheme, but it will severely tax the organisational ability of a company which embarks on such a plan. Experience suggests that only partial success is normally obtained in the pursuit of a complete and totally reconcilable database. The user management will tend to remain sceptical of any information system which is based upon the use of inconsistent data, and yet they may not wish to commit a large amount of their own energy to control the data needed in the database.

Figure 6.1   *Basic concept of an MIS.*

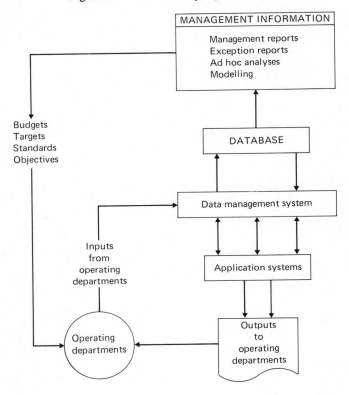

COHERENCE WITHIN THE DATABASE

1   Responsibility for Data
A manager directly responsible for a particular operational department can be expected to take responsibility for the data that is used within his operation, to understand it, and to co-operate with the system designers in the development of systems to support his function. For more senior levels of management, the information requirements of an individual manager are more generalised. Three particular problems manifest themselves:

(a)   A senior manager will be less familiar with the detail behind any

100

figures presented and will have to rely upon the control exerted by others to monitor the quality of information provided. It may not be easy for such a person to detect mistakes in the information supplied to him, and he may recommend disastrous courses of action based upon incorrect information, or upon incorrect understanding of the information.

(b) Such a manager may also receive information emanating from different units within the organisation, and will be frustrated and dismayed by any contradictions displayed by the data. Feeling powerless in the face of such confusion, he may give up trying to use the system and will have to make judgements without knowing the real facts.

(c) In a large and complex information system, it will not be easy for individual managers to appreciate the precise meaning of information and the many ways in which data may be classified by the system. They may misinterpret the information presented, or not appreciate the full potential contained therein.

All of these problems can be met by policies pertaining to the control of data. Data must be regarded as a valuable asset to the company.

As a first step, a rigorous attitude must be adopted towards controlling all the data applied to the files, and for validating it and correcting any inconsistencies that arise. A system of control has to be maintained to prove that the files have been correctly updated, and any output selected from the files must include control information to enable it to be balanced back to the original file. This is a fundamental principle of any data processing system, but it becomes more complex when one is dealing with a database which is updated and utilised by several independent departments.

Superficially, it appears necessary to establish a central data control function to co-ordinate this activity, but since such a unit has no real operational role within the group as a whole, it may find itself on the receiving end of bad data originating from the departments having operational responsibility for the generation of such data. This provides great potential for organisational conflict, and sometimes results in the situation where responsibility for the accuracy of the files falls uneasily between different areas of the company. This leads to some golden rules for MIS implementation:

Rule 1: Always make sure that the responsibility for the accuracy of data in particular files of the database is clearly vested in a particular department which has an operational interest in its accuracy.

Rule 2: The department concerned should be the primary generator and user of the basic data and should appoint a file controller whose role involves the routine collection and validation of the data.

Rule 3: Other departments having a secondary role must be prepared to support the file controller appointed by the primary department.

101

Rule 4: Budgets for carrying out data-control tasks must be rationally evaluated, and departments must be given resources to carry out work in accordance with the standards implied by the quality and type of information required by users.

Rule 5: Requests from users for information from the database should be received by the file controller whose job it will be to interpret each request and control the quality of output.

By appointing file controllers who will be responsible for particular files, it is possible to deal with the three problems identified at the beginning of this section:

(a) The file controller and his staff are responsible for the maintenance of adequate controls to verify the completeness and accuracy of any output produced as a sub-set of the file.

(b) A file controller will be responsible for all data of a given type and for co-ordinating the maintenance of a single file to contain all such data. Thus one of his prime objectives is to work with the systems development staff to eliminate disparate sources of information.

(c) The file controller and his staff will also vet each request for information to decide objectively whether the quality of information is sufficiently good to yield a beneficial output to the users.

To succeed in any MIS implementation, file controllers must receive the full support of the top management and line managers with whom they are involved. They must be able to see their job as being above the parochial interests of their local department and must have a highly developed ability for lateral communication within the organisation.

If these attitudes cannot be inspired within the organisation, then there is little hope of achieving an information system which provides accurate and compatible information across the organisation. All the money and skill applied to the design of such a system will be wasted, and the management will perhaps benefit more from projects dedicated to specific problem areas within particular departments.

Figure 6.2 shows an organisation chart which suggests a method of organising the file control responsibilities. It is an example taken from International Computers Limited, where for a number of years I was responsible for the design and development of an integrated management information system.

In the diagram, I have shown three files only and demonstrated how the lines of communication were organised to involve several departments in the creation and maintenance of these files. Individual file controllers reported to a central database administrator who co-ordinated their activities and supported them in creating the database in accordance with the needs of the group.

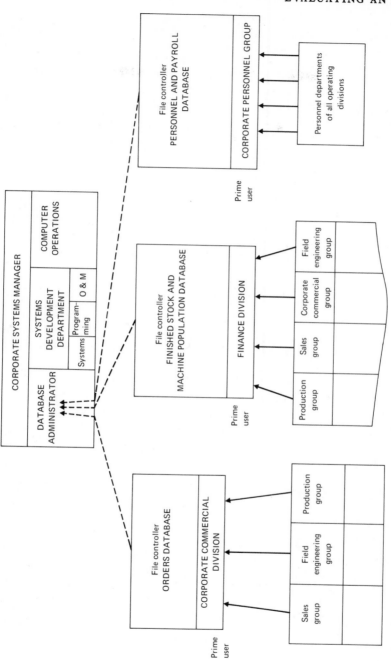

Figure 6.2 *Organisation of data control for MIS*

2   Compatible Coding Systems

The gradual integration of an organisation's procedures and systems will be a long and gradual process. It will only be possible to create a mutually compatible file system if the information in the various files is based upon a uniform coding structure which will enable data from different parts of the company to be matched and collated.

It is probable that the local procedures and systems which have been developed prior to the decision to build an MIS will not use compatible code structures. For example, a manufacturing organisation decided to set up a central purchasing system to achieve the benefits of bulk purchases. This company had five major manufacturing centres which had previously developed independent production control systems. The following problems had to be overcome:

(a)   Each centre had independent name and address files for suppliers.
(b)   Each centre had different codes to identify the suppliers and the different addresses from which suppliers operated.
(c)   Individual components were primarily identified by numeric codes developed separately for the convenience of local production methods.
(d)   The use of component codes originated by the suppliers was not of a consistent quality at each centre.

There is no quick solution to such a set of problems. Painstaking work involving the systems development staff and data control staff in the different centres was necessary, and a file controller had to be appointed to be responsible for the central system and for co-ordinating the gradual elimination of the local systems. A number of central files and indexes had to be established including:

(a)   A single suppliers file to record all the standard information required about suppliers.
(b)   A single code for each supplier and a system of sub-codes to identify the different addresses from which they operated.
(c)   Standard numeric codes to describe components and their precise dimensions and values. (This also led to a system which enabled control to be exercised over the variety of components used in new products.)
(d)   An improvement in the use made of component codes originated by suppliers.

As these central files were established, the local files had to be amended and maintained to the same standard, until eventually all the data could be merged together into a central system and the local systems abandoned.

The benefits of the centralised system were, in this example, not difficult to predict. It still needed a collective will on the part of the different people involved to push this project through to success. Local centres were particularly reluctant to adopt the new coding structures because it caused them much temporary instability throughout the long and difficult development period.

This kind of problem is familiar in any data processing project, but it is ever-present in the development of a database to serve an organisation's total management information needs. The management involved in these issues must support the development and introduction of consistent code structures, and the responsibility for the design of such codes should rest with the central systems development unit.

It is impossible to achieve a truly integrated management information system without a concentration of effort on these matters. If the top management are not prepared to support such efforts, then the attempt to build an MIS will be futile.

RESPONSE REQUIRED BY MANAGEMENT

1   Adaptability of Systems to Management Needs

A management information system must be responsive to the management that it serves. This must be evident in the way in which routine operational systems are operated; it must be possible to adapt systems to meet the demands of new business situations. It is not good enough to persuade managers to defer the introduction of new policies and techniques simply because the computer department cannot cope with the workload entailed in amending existing systems. Unhappily, this is an excuse frequently encountered within commercial and industrial life.

There are two concepts which the forward-looking management services manager will need to observe to preserve the adaptability of his organisation's management information system. These precepts are associated with database management, a subject dealt with in some detail in Chapter 7. It is necessary to introduce them into our discussion at this stage to stress their importance in achieving the essential characteristics of being flexible:

(a)   Transparency of the database.
(b)   Data management languages.

Transparency implies that the data files are structured in a manner which enables them to be enlarged and extended in format and scope without requiring all existing routines that may use those files to be amended. In effect, a programmer writes his programs to call for specific classes of records, and fields within records, without necessarily knowing precisely how the data in the files is organised. Software forming part of the database management system takes care of the interface needed between applications programs and the database files. Programmers who are developing application programs are able to update and retrieve data from the database according to the needs of their application and regardless of other applications that may use the files.

105

A general-purpose data management language has the advantage that it will enable programmers to develop and amend routines in less time than if a procedural language, such as COBOL, were used. The functions permitted using such languages within data management systems include file creation, validation, file restructuring, file updating and interrogation. Functions available within such languages are pre-programmed generalised routines available to the user without having to write detailed coding. There are a number of such languages now in commercial use.

In many cases, it is claimed that such languages enabled managers, and other non-data processing specialists, to directly interrogate the database. Such claims are usually exaggerated, and even where non-specialists are able to use such languages, it is often necessary to restrict use to a sub-set of the facilities available and to a limited range of data elements. However, we must acknowledge that one objective of the computer staff must be to realise a wider use of the database, and use by non-specialist staff has to be encouraged.

A significant part of the problem is centred around the sheer complexity of a large database, the number of data elements within it, and the ability of individual managers and line staff to understand the full significance of the data. This underlines the role ascribed to file controllers, i.e. their involvement with users in the exploitation of the database and as interpreters and quality controllers of information provided to users.

2   Response in Provision of Ad Hoc Information

If we accept that systems can be designed to be flexible and adaptable to a changing environment, it follows that they will contain information which managers will grow to rely on increasingly. This will lead to the desire to make more non-routine inquiries of the system. Bearing in mind the difficulties discussed above concerning the potential complexity of the database, we now have to deal with a number of problems affecting access to the data.

A manager who works closely with certain segments of information will eventually grow to understand the database. He will know the quality of the information that can be generated, and will know how much trust can be placed upon it. He will also get to know the code structures which help him to comprehend the analyses that can be obtained, and be able to appreciate the significance of potential results. Such an awareness can be developed only over a period of involvement with the designers of the system, and it is most likely that the assistance of the designers and file controllers will always be needed to exploit the database effectively on behalf of management. With a very large generalised database, such assistance will need to be an on-going commitment requiring particular recognition in the organisation of the systems development unit. Typically, a manager will expect to request information to solve a particular problem and be helped by the systems development staff who will have to understand his problem, identify relevant data which can be used to meet the requirement,

106

and develop computer procedures to extract relevant data from the files and output the information.

Except in predetermined cases, managers will not usually be able to interrogate the database directly. The potential hazards of misinterpreting the information, or of failing to appreciate the standards and methods of quality control which are necessary, weigh strongly in favour of some specialised technical support which must provide the following:

(a) Analyse requests for information to evaluate whether it can be provided from the existing database; check also whether the user is authorised to receive output from the file.

(b) Identify any relevant shortcomings in the current data which are likely to prejudice the value of the results.

(c) Evaluate how the request can be met and prepare the necessary programs or parameters to produce the desired results.

(d) Schedule the production of the information and advise the user of the time needed to prepare the answer and the costs entailed.

(e) Check whether the inquiry will produce an unreasonable volume of output; work with the user to design an output report which is concise yet sufficiently detailed for his needs.

(f) Design control totals and procedures to check the credibility and accuracy of the output against control figures routinely maintained for the database.

(g) Produce the results, check the quality, and hand over to the user and help him interpret the answer where necessary.

An examination of these tasks leads to the conclusion that file controllers and programming staff must be involved in this activity. One can also see that *instant* answers to users' requests for information are not always practicable. It may take anything from a few hours to many days to answer a particular request.

It is clear that, for full exploitation of a database, the data processing management must be prepared to dedicate a considerable volume of manpower to ad hoc programming activity, and that it will be difficult to decide in advance how much of this activity is really worthwhile.

As a general principle, it is important to charge user departments with all the costs associated with undertaking ad hoc activities on their behalf. In this way, they are persuaded to evaluate the benefits obtained from using these resources, and, in the long run, their demands will be rationalised.

A management information system is a valuable tool if it provides a service in helping management to formulate better strategies and take decisions which could not otherwise be made. If resources are not available to meet the needs of managers, the management information system cannot be effectively exploited and it may fall into disrepute. If checks are not placed upon indiscriminate use of the system and accompanying resources, a mass of useless and very expensive reports may result to overload the computer department, and inflate its budget unnecessarily.

SUMMARY OF CHAPTER 6

I have attempted in this chapter to identify the organisational problems which are encountered frequently in MIS implementation. Policies must be established by top management to create an environment in which these problems can be resolved. If these problems are left to be tackled by the management services manager in isolation, the MIS is liable to be extremely expensive and ineffective, except in isolated parts where an understanding user manager may show insight in fostering the right attitudes. Below I have summarised the attitudes to be adopted and suggested outline policies for successful MIS implementation.

1   The implementation of a management information system is a complex task requiring a great deal of understanding and support by management.
2   By definition, an MIS must support all the major operating units and the top management, and be capable of rapid extension and adaptation to meet their changing requirements.
3   Although some aspects of the system will support operational units where cost/benefits can be readily evaluated, many of the sub-systems will be difficult to justify in economic terms.
4   There are often considerable benefits in improving the accuracy and consistency of an organisation's data. This, in itself, may lead to improved control over assets and revenue.
5   An MIS must be able to support management in dealing with non-routine situations by providing ad hoc analyses and reports. Such reports are expensive to produce. Costs should be charged to the users in order to encourage them to evaluate the benefits obtained and, by experience, to establish appropriate uses of the system.
6   The integration of an organisation's procedures into an MIS will eventually result in more consistent information for top management, giving them a better environment for making important policy decisions.
7   An MIS must contain data which is accurate, relevant and up to date, and reflect current events within the company and its real-world environment.
8   Information has to be up to date, but this does not imply that files are updated in real-time. Information must be sufficiently up to date to support the requirements of the individual users. The important criterion is that accurate information must be provided in sufficient time to enable individual users to take controlling action within their functional responsibilities.
9   There must be an overall plan for the rationalisation of data which is approved and supported by management. Such a plan requires the

reorganising of most of the basic procedures which support the organisation's operations.

10   The data processing unit should not be expected to take responsibility for the day-to-day control of data in user departments.

11   Database controllers should be appointed in appropriate user departments to control and co-ordinate the development and maintenance of accurate data.

12   Budgets should be developed to allow database controllers the resources to discharge these responsibilities.

13   Database controllers can also vet requests for information and assist management in interpreting their requirements and the results produced.

14   The codes and data structures in use within an organisation will require revision to ensure that systems are mutually coherent. This may entail disruption and change in working methods in departments which may not receive an immediate benefit. The management must be prepared to support this sort of activity.

15   The data processing department must be prepared to design flexible systems using data management techniques, and use high-level programming languages to minimise the programming effort required in responding to management's requirements.

16   In some cases, managers and their operating staff can be provided with terminals to interrogate the database directly.

17   If the database is large and the file structure complex, it is more practical to restrict terminals for use of only selected users upon parts of the database.

18   The majority of ad hoc requirements will have to be met by use of programming staff and file controllers, and managers must be prepared to pay for such technical assistance if they wish to enjoy support in non-routine situations.

19   Development of systems within an MIS environment will be more complex than developing individual systems. The cost/benefits will be more difficult to predict.

20   The decision to implement an MIS must be taken at the highest level. The management must be prepared to face considerable problems in organisation and communication, particularly if their MIS embraces many separate but adjacent procedures rather than a large dedicated application.

Chapter 7

Is Database Management Worth the Investment?

In the preceding chapter, I have identified the task facing management in implementing an MIS: it is a considerable one, but worth pursuing if your organisation is suffering from a confusing and contradictory array of systems. The implications of going ahead with a full MIS are a substantial degree of technical, managerial and clerical effort. It is usually safest to restrict the MIS approach to selected areas of the database, and to work in an evolutionary manner to expand and extend it.

This may require the use of a data management system. Some database management systems (DMS) are very substantial items of software and will result in expensive overheads in the operation of applications. These overheads are of two types:

(a) Use of more core store and other hardware resources.
(b) More time required in execution of the users' application routines.

At the end of this chapter we will return to these matters, but first we will discuss the nature of a database system, the features which have to be observed in the technical design, and the reason why these features are important.

The Essential Nature of a Database
In an MIS we start off with the fundamental situation of having a database shared by many application programs. Data emanating from the operations of the company is collected, validated, edited and consolidated into files which are used by the application programs as and when required. The data in the files would initially be organised to present a most efficient method of operation within the computer, and to allow as much flexibility as possible for future changes and for the later needs of further applications.

Since particular applications will require only a sub-set of the data at any moment in time, there is a tendency to require direct access storage devices for master files, and to employ methods of retrieval which will extract application sub-files from the database whenever required. The retrieval techniques will be designed to enable the application of files to be created without necessarily searching through the whole of the master files concerned; this is important because master files will consist of as many records and data elements as are required by all the applications. For efficiency, therefore, the system must allow for the selection of records by various criteria, without the necessity of examining every record in the file.

The basic unit of data organisation will normally be a single record for each entity. For example, in a master file concerned with employees there will be one record per individual and each record will be identified by a unique key, e.g. the personnel number. The selection criteria for different applications might include age, sex, grade, salary, length of service, job title, date of next salary review, performance level, qualifications and so on.

All user departments will update the same record, e.g. in the case of a personnel file, the payroll department, personnel administration department, pensions department and the local managers of the departments directly responsible for employees. The different functions performed by these departments will dictate the type and accuracy of data elements required on the master file, but the information will need to be organised independently of any particular application requirements. Of course, the methods for representing individual data elements must be common to all applications.

As far as possible, applications should be designed to make the user departments dependent upon the system and dependent upon one another. Thus an event recorded by one user will automatically generate documentation or signals to cause other departments to take action. In this way, users are obliged to co-operate in the accurate maintenance of the database and the total system is really able to provide a central co-ordinating function.

Relationship between File Structure and Applications

In any system, the intention is to design a file structure which is consistent with the output required, and yet which minimises the amount of computer time required to run the application as a whole. In a database designed to meet the changing requirements of many applications, the system designer is obliged to consider flexibility above almost everything else, and efficiency, while being still important, inevitably has less influence on the design of any particular application. The overall system is designed to be as efficient as practicable to support the initial applications, and to permit other applications to be developed later.

Individual applications will usually require only some of the records in the database. Also, the criteria for selecting records from the database will be different for different applications, and it follows that the database has to be structured to enable different sub-sets of records to be readily extracted. The easy retrieval of information is one of the essential attributes

111

of a management information system, and the functions involved in this process should allow for the extraction of records representing a desired sub-set of the database and the collation, sequencing, and presentation of sub-sets of information to show selected individual records or summarised data from chosen sets of records.

A database management system is designed to facilitate this process by providing a file handling routine which controls the selection of data from the database files, making information available to individual application

Figure 7.1   *Data management and file handling.*

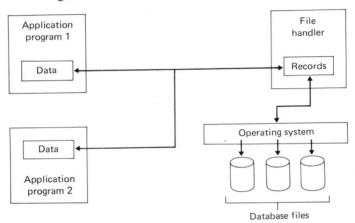

programs, as shown in Figure 7.1. In the simplest situation, the application program indicates the particular records required by nominating the keys of individual records and specifying the particular data elements from the records required for use in the application.

However, not all applications will require such a simple method of selection. For example, an inquiry program may require the following data from a personnel file:

all records which concern,
      male employees
      under 35 years of age
      with accounting qualifications
      who are unmarried
      can speak French
      in salary scale £2,500 to £3,500
      trained in systems analysis techniques

Assuming that all these attributes are represented by codes held on the records, it is possible for them to be selected by the file handler. It could

112

search through the records to identify those which conform to the requirements. However, this approach would be expensive and time-consuming, each record having to be read into main memory and examined to see whether it meets the requirements in order to create a sub-file for use by the application.

This type of inquiry is often best handled by maintaining, in addition to the main file, an inverted file, i.e. one which is organised as a list of attributes which provide pointers to the records which contain these attributes.

Figure 7.2 *Retrieval of records by pre-selection of attributes.*

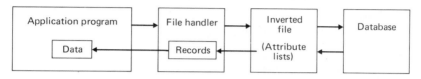

Attribute lists will be concise and capable of rapid interrogation without excessive costs in computer time. In this way, it is possible economically to pre-select the records desired without having to search through the whole main file (see Figure 7.2).

This technique is useful to retrieval purposes, but it presents its problems to the system designer in that file maintenance becomes a much more complicated process. For example, every time a field in a record is amended, the program which performs the amendment has also to amend the attribute lists in the inverted file, and this may entail re-sequencing the lists in order to be ready for a subsequent interrogation. This is a typical situation in database management – advantages gained in one direction may be costly in another.

There are many other ways of organising files and retrieval techniques, and it is not our place to examine these methods in detail here. However, it remains generally true that no single file structure will provide a solution to the problem of data organisation in a generalised database. Whatever else a complex file organisation may provide, it will cause some applications to incur overheads in maintaining indexes and searching for records. Additional storage may also be necessary to store information to assist in selection and general housekeeping.

As far as practicable, one must design the file structure to be as efficient as possible when used by those applications which require most frequent activity, and which handle large volumes of data. Efficiency is not so important in applications which are run infrequently.

Sometimes the requirements of applications are so different that it is not feasible to utilise a common method of file organisation. The file then has to be reorganised before carrying out certain applications. In these circumstances, it is desirable to ensure that the main updating process takes place on a particular version of the file, and that such other files as may be created from time to time are simply different expressions of the same basic data and have a transient existence to service particular applications only.

Transparency: Independence of Data

We have seen that a database has to be developed in an evolutionary manner as the MIS which it supports is extended to further areas of the business. A database management system may allow for different file media to be used throughout the evolution of a particular file. The individual application programs which use the file must also be made independent of the physical file structure prevailing at the time if we are to avoid continually rewriting application programs as the MIS is extended. Within certain limitations, such independence can be achieved by use of file-handling software forming part of a database management system.

For this to be possible, there has to be a separate description stored within the data management system for each database file. The records and data elements which comprise the file must also be specified by this method. This description amounts to an index, or data definition, describing the files and individual data elements and the hierarchical relationship contained therein. It is itself stored as a file on the backing store within the computer, perhaps as part of the file that it describes.

The descriptor contains all the details required to specify the file, its method of organisation and content. Individual application programs which require access to data from the files do not need to specify the structure of the file and its records, but simply call for data, identified by common data names, to be provided by the file handler. The file handler in turn interprets such requests and uses the descriptor to identify and select physical records from the files and present the application program with just the data it requires.

This means that the file structure can be changed, fields can be added to a file, or be deleted from a file, without necessarily affecting all those application programs which use the files. Thus the file itself can be developed and extended over a period of time without amending existing programs. The time and money invested in the development of the initial applications will not be jeopardised by further enhancements of the database.

This sort of flexibility is crucial in the development of a database, and the word 'transparency' has been coined to describe this condition of independence between the application programs and physical database organisation.

Are there limitations to this flexibility? In practice, there are:

(a) In the first place, if field sizes or formats of individual data elements are altered, then programs using these fields must be amended.
(b) Some programs must change if the order or hierarchical structure of a file is changed.

It is also necessary to organise a system whereby common names are used to identify data elements in all programs which use the database. These data names will need to be in general use by systems and programming staff throughout the organisation, and standards must be published which define the structure, format and range of values that particular data elements may take.

General Features of Database Management Systems

Database management systems have been developed in response to the need for greater flexibility and resilience in computer applications. That the need is real cannot be denied. The circumstantial evidence points overwhelmingly to a high degree of obsolescence in applications developed by most computer users.

Technically, DMS systems are proving to be effective, but some cause for concern must be felt for the overheads which they demand. For example, a typical data management system might require a processor with a minimum of 64,000 words of immediate access store in order to support implementation. The individual routines in such a system may impose considerable overheads in running time during operation of an application.

It is difficult to be specific about this, outside a given application. The file-handling properties of a DMS will, as we have seen, enable an application program to request a logical file to be provided from a number of physical files stored in the database. The efficiency with which this can be performed is affected by the relationship between the data requested by an application and the physical distribution of that data across physical files. The sequence and structure of the physical files plays an important part in this, as does the nature and complexity of any indexes established to assist in information retrieval. Complex file structures based upon networks are one method used to mitigate some of the difficulties described here (see Figure 7.3).

Figure 7.3   *A file structure network.*

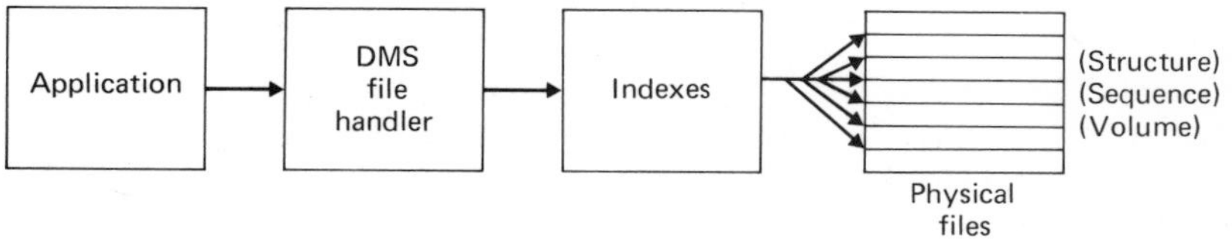

Most DMS systems contain facilities which need only be implemented if desired, and the software system itself can be considered as a series of modules which provide these different facilities. This, of course, helps to minimise unnecessary overheads, but even so, the size of the basic facilities needed in a DMS will usually preclude its use for a wide range of smaller users.

115

Let us now look at some of the facilities and comment on their relevance and importance.

Data Management Languages
One of the most important requirements of a data management system is the need to make both programmers and systems staff more productive and to reduce the time required by them to set up and implement a new computer procedure. The use of high-level data management languages provides this benefit. Most of the routines required in any application can be pre-programmed as generalised routines which, when supplied with specific parameters within a given application, can perform specific operations.

The programmer has less control over the detailed steps in a procedure since he is effectively providing parameters to link together and drive a series of pre-programmed modules. The routines thus constructed carry out major file processing functions such as:

(a) File creation.
(b) File comparison.
(c) Input validation.
(d) File restructuring.
(e) File updating.
(f) Interrogation (including selection, retrieval, arrangement and reporting).

The use of these methods enables computer procedures to be developed quickly; and it can also be used to create ad hoc computer procedures, such as those required for file building system development, or for non-routine reporting from operational systems.

The great disadvantage in using these techniques is the machine time required in running applications. A specially tailored system in assembly language or COBOL can be more efficient once it is operational. However, there is no doubt that the ability to develop new procedures quickly and accurately is an important benefit and is an essential feature of a DMS.

Complex File Structures
The tendency towards complex file structures is encouraged by the need physically to structure the data so that elements in different logical sets can be related over a wide range of applications. A network structure of the type shown in Figure 7.4 illustrates the principles.

Where networks, or linkages, are not established to cross-reference logical sets of data, such references would have to be established by re-sequencing separate files and comparing them one with another to match records having common keys, i.e. a very time-consuming and expensive approach.

However, complex file structures can be much more difficult to create and update, and the various applications may incur time overheads in the

116

updating phase of operation. Complex files may need much more sophisticated procedures to provide protection against corruption of data, e.g. by
unauthorised action of a program upon certain data elements which it must
not be permitted to amend. Procedures to recover from hardware on software failure will also need to be more luxurious in the case of complex files
rather than with standard serial or sequentially organised files.

Figure 7.4   *Example of a complex file structure in database management.*

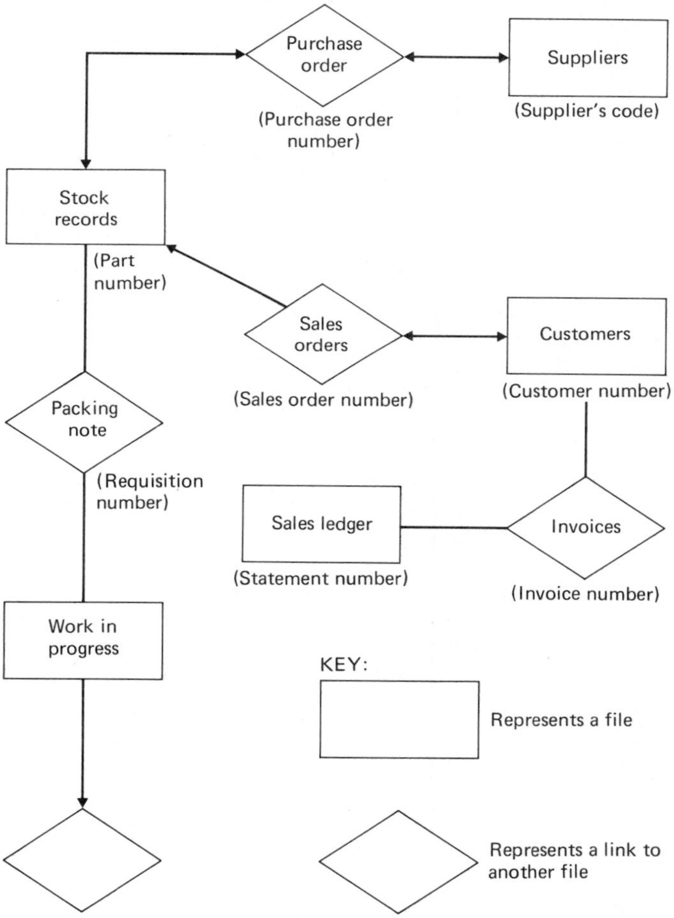

Privacy of Data

Some DMS systems have elaborate facilities to prevent unauthorised access
to data. Data containing personal details of individuals obviously must be

117

secure, as must data which can carry secret or confidential information about the organisation and its performance.

Privacy facilities can be such as to provide control over individual fields, both to inhibit unauthorised access and to log attempts by users to do so. The need for this degree of control must depend upon the circumstances prevailing in the organisation and the nature of the application. To a great extent, simple manual procedures and checks upon the authority of those users who request information can cater for the level of screening necessary.

Perhaps rigorous privacy facilities are essential in giving confidence to managers who are being coerced into giving up their own local systems to collaborate in the creation and maintenance of a database. In practice, it can be observed that successful implementation of a database will encourage the growth of more objective and open attitudes to the use of management information. Hopefully, the need for rigorous privacy facilities can be restricted to those applications which truly justify it.

A Simple Approach to Data Management
In the earlier sections, I have mentioned the considerable overheads that can be incurred in using large general-purpose data management systems. These overheads will tend to increase the cost of running individual applications and result in a less efficient use of computer hardware. It is tempting to say that these data management systems are expensive luxuries, or follies of the computer era. Personally, I do not hold with this view, but I would examine the relevance of such systems to any organisation cautiously before recommending their use.

The main benefits that we seek in using data management techniques are:

(a) An ability to create files which can be gradually extended for use in all relevant areas of the organisation, thus providing a reliable and consistent source of information for management.
(b) An independence between the file structure and application programs using files so that files can be developed without heavy penalties in re-programming original applications.
(c) An ability to withstand changes needed to respond to movements in the external organisation of the business.

If we analyse these needs, it is evident that they are relevant to all classes of user in the commercial and industrial field, and are not simply restricted to organisations who have aimed specifically at a total management information system. Therefore we should always seek methods of achieving these benefits.

The systems approach to this problem tells us that we should isolate the factors which are susceptible to change and not embed them deep in the logic of our application programs. Instead, the programs should be structured in accord with rigorous standards which permit input formats, file structures and output formats to be amended without the need seriously to disturb the code of the application programs. One method of achieving this is to represent these features of the application by tables stored as part of the program, which can themselves be amended by parameters whenever changes are necessary.

Figure 7.5   *A simple approach to data management.*

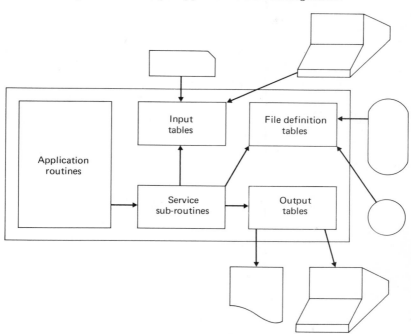

Figure 7.5 illustrates the principles involved. Basically, the technique is concerned with increasing the flexibility of application programs.

To consider how this works, let us consider the case of input: transactions received by the applications program will be identified as being of particular types. Each type will be represented by a description stored in the input table. The description itself will tell the application program all it needs to know about each type of transaction, including:

(a)   The media used.
(b)   Number of data elements and their identity.
(c)   Their size and structure.
(d)   The position of fields.
(e)   Validation rules.
(f)   Editing requirements.

119

Such details can be specified concisely as entries in a table, and these entries are interpreted at run time by the application program as it deals with each transaction. The overheads are minimal, if not non-existent, since the space occupied by the entries in the table will be comparable with that otherwise occupied by the coding in the application routines, and processing by means of internally stored tables is very efficient.

The output tables provide similar functions for all types of output; and the tables which define files provide for the definition of file and data structures independently from the application programs.

The service sub-routines shown in Figure 7.5 are for data manipulation functions common to most applications, and are available to the application by reference to the relevant tables.

This technique represents a standard approach to application design which formalises the way in which the application designer approaches his task. The principles can be used throughout all systems which are predominantly of the information-handling type, and will lead to an improvement in the control of application development besides imparting a resilience to changes in the real-world environment. The benefits may be summarised as follows:

(a) The concept of transparency is afforded by the separation of application coding and data definition.
(b) Systems can be developed which will be resilient to changing requirements.
(c) Changes during and after implementation can be accepted without the need constantly to rewrite previous application coding.
(d) Standard systems can be developed for general application with a high degree of tolerance to different environments.
(e) The essential ingredients of data management are available without the costly overheads imposed by some large data management systems.
(f) Standards are imposed which enhance management control over application development.
(g) The techniques can be applied in real-time and batch processing systems with a wide variety of input and output devices.
(h) Ad hoc reports can be readily created.

The Need for Database Management
If an organisation decides to develop an MIS, then some form of database management system is essential. If the management are prepared to grapple with the organisational problems and policies needed effectively to introduce an MIS, as described in the previous chapter, then they will not begrudge the additional facilities needed effectively to manage the database. Let it be understood that the more complex the facilities are from a particular data management system, the more expensive it is in terms of the hardware overheads needed. Yet DMS systems have their place: they

120

enable systems analysts and programmers to cope with change and to contain the complexities imposed in MIS situations, *but* they do not enable us to dispense with the disciplines suggested in the previous chapter.

What I have tried to do in this chapter is to put DMS into perspective. Almost any organisation which is growing and evolving in a real-world situation will have a requirement for building systems which can evolve and be responsive to management. In practice, almost every organisation will have need of a database, but not everyone can afford to employ a large database management system. This is a matter to be determined by examination of a specific organisation's problems.

SUMMARY OF CHAPTER 7

1 A data management system is an essential tool for the technical staff involved in the development and maintenance of a database for an MIS system.

2 It gives the data processing people a greater degree of flexibility in providing information systems which are capable of being adapted to respond to the changing business environment.

3 A database management system allows for the use of complex file structures; and methods of file maintenance and information retrieval which facilitate the integration of applications.

4 Although the technical attributes of data management systems are very important for MIS, they do not release management from the need for a disciplined attitude towards the control of data.

5 Typically, data management systems are not for the small user, and considerable overhead costs may be incurred when using such systems.

6 Careful selection of the facilities offered by DMS software may help to mitigate these overheads – but don't expect to get the full benefits of DMS without costs.

7 It is possible, in some circumstances, to develop systems which are tolerant to change without using a large DMS utility. This can be achieved by structuring programs to rigorous standards which enable input, output and file structures to be amended without disturbing the detailed logic of the application programs.

8 The needs for DMS can only be considered for a particular organisation in the light of prevailing circumstances. The hardware utilisation costs of DMS may be from 15 per cent to 100 per cent in excess of normal costs. The choice must depend upon this factor, plus consideration of the benefits imposed by an integrated information system.

Chapter 8

Controlling the Costs of Software Agencies

There has been a considerable growth in the software services industry in recent years, and many organisations today entrust the development of their computer systems to outside agencies. There is much to be said in favour of this, particularly for small organisations who do not wish to develop career structures for data processing staff within their own organisations. There are many such companies who have significant data processing loads and have a substantial financial turnover, but have staff numbers measured in hundreds rather than thousands. Examples include stockbrokers, merchant banks and insurance brokers.

Such companies will seek to obtain professional assistance in establishing and running their computer systems, and they may initially do this by using a computer bureau. Eventually the company will grow large enough to buy or lease a computer. When this happens, they are faced with the problem of deciding whether to develop their computer system themselves or subcontract the work to a software house. Even companies with very large computer departments will use the services of a software house, particularly to meet peak loads and to cover staff shortages, but most often to buy specific expertise or to obtain assurance that a particular project will be implemented on time.

Most software houses will charge fees which are equivalent to two and a half to three times the salary cost of the staff working on projects. This level of charging allows them their profit, covers the overhead costs of the operation, and covers also the idle time when staff are being trained or otherwise not earning revenue. It is obviously an expensive matter to allow a software house to undertake a project for your organisation without monitoring their activity carefully to ensure that costs are contained and objectives are met. It is often true that companies cause themselves unnecessary expenditure and time in implementing projects because they fail to establish a sound working basis with their software supplier, and do not take decisions in a timely way. Remember, in data processing *lost time is very expensive.* In this chapter I have set down some basic ground rules for working with a software agency, so that the purchaser will know what to expect from the agency and know also what his own commitment should be to ensure success.

Terms of Reference and Commercial Basis
It is clearly advisable to generate detailed terms of reference for all agency staff so that the work to be performed can be evaluated and measured and a suitable commercial basis be established between the buyer and the software house. The problem with most computer projects is that it is often not practical for the full complexity of the work to be realised at the very beginning, and also that both parties are dependent upon one another in many detailed ways during the course of the project. The contract therefore has to distinguish clear contractual milestones and responsibilities during the course of the project. Figure 8.1 indicates the primary stages in a project and the suggested commercial basis for each stage.

Figure 8.1   *Commercial arrangements in projects contracted to software agencies.*

Stage	Charging basis
1 Definition of requirements	Time and materials
2 Systems specification	Time and materials
3 Programming specification	Fixed price
4 Programming	Fixed price
5 Trials and implementation	Time and materials
6 Support and maintenance	Fee plus time and materials

Of course, the objective of the purchaser in contract negotiation, is to obtain a fixed price and a fixed and agreed implementation date for all stages of the project. The software house will attempt to avoid specific constraints or fixed price commitments in order to minimise the effects of a project which overruns.

The principle costs of the project to the vendor will include:

(a)   Manpower.
(b)   Computer time.
(c)   Expenses in travelling to and operating at the customer's site.

A small project – one entailing, say, about 50 to 100 man/weeks of effort – will be more easily evaluated and priced than a larger project. It is possible that the requirement can be evaluated and a quotation produced in two to three weeks, allowing both parties to agree the price and timescale at the beginning. However, the software house will usually specify activities which the purchaser must provide to ensure timely completion, and may reserve the right to charge for delays and idle time incurred resulting from failure to complete these activities. The following items may be included in this list:

123

(a) Availability of customer's staff for fact gathering and decision making.
(b) Approval of functional requirements and design specifications within specified times from presentation of such documents.
(c) Preparation of test data for the system.
(d) Availability of user's staff to implement and run the system live.

The staged approach to the contract suggested in Figure 10.1 (page 146) allows the phases to be separated into :

(a) Activities in which the software agency is dependent upon detailed collaboration with the customer.
(b) Activities which are the software agency's sole responsibility.

In the former case, it is customary to charge fees according to time and materials expended; and in the latter case, it is common practice to agree a fixed-price contract.

A complete contract may therefore involve a number of commercial agreements allowing the parties to agree terms at the completion of each stage before starting the next phase. To the software supplier, this is good, since it minimises the risks and allows each stage to be approached coolly after due reflection upon the experience gained to date. From the purchaser's point of view, there are distinct disadvantages :

(a) The final cost of the project grows as each stage is opened up for detailed scheduling and evaluation; thus it becomes difficult to anticipate the true costs when creating the initial project budget.
(b) The software supplier can gradually inflate the price as the project proceeds, and the purchaser may find it difficult to resist the supplier upon whom he has become dependent for delivery of his system.

However, a lot can be done to avoid these dangers and to establish a pattern of working which is fair to both parties.

Key Requirements for Agreeing a Software Contract
First of all, the purchaser should allow the software supplier sufficient time to study his problem so that a budgetary estimate and an outline design can be produced. This estimate should be written into the contract, showing the expected costs of each stage and placing responsibility upon the software supplier to justify any departures from those costs in subsequent stages. The initial quotation should be supported by detailed schedules of resources required at each stage and the rates of charge used for recovering fees for these resources. The vendor is thus compelled to justify the proposed cost of all stages whether they entail fixed-price commitments or not.

Of course, there is nothing like competition to create a keen price, but one should beware of asking too many vendors to quote. It is very difficult to be sure that they are all given sufficient opportunity to familiarise with the job in hand, and this may place a strain upon the time which you, as the purchaser, are able to devote to their various questions and approaches. It is also important to ensure that quotations are produced on a comparable basis; and, if possible, a tender specification should be produced specifying the level of detail expected from each of the software vendors in their quotations.

It is not always advisable to look for the cheapest quotation, and it is well worth checking the 'track record' of organisations answering your tender. Ask them for details of previous contracts which are comparable with your own, and check these out by contacting the customers concerned. The kind of actions which you should take to satisfy yourself that you are dealing with a good organisation include :

(a)   Assess the quality of staff by examining career résumés and records of experience.
(b)   Find out how many people are in the organisation and whether their commitments are such that they are available to do your work .
(c)   Select those who have experience relevant to your problems and visit the vendor's site to interview the staff.
(d)   Ask for named people to be committed to your project, particularly for key roles.
(e)   Make sure the project manager has a previous background of success, and that he will be available to give a full-time commitment to your project.
(f)   Assess, if practicable, whether the vendor is financially secure.

The vendor will equally look for commitments from you in return, e.g. an early decision to justify earmarking named people; a willingness on your part to pay for the services of the project manager on a full-time basis throughout.

Standards

A most vital part of any software system is the documentation that describes it. The vendor should be asked to provide copies of his documentation standards for systems investigation and design, program specification and completed program documentation. References should be taken up to see that the documentation standards are applied in practice.

The methods of project management and the standards used for estimating and recording progress against estimates should be examined.

In addition, formal ground rules for running progress meetings, and for documenting communications between vendor and purchaser, should be agreed. A formal procedure must be established to review the project and to issue system change notes and evaluate their implications for the project. These procedures will need to be agreed before the contract is ultimately signed, but it is useful to explore the software supplier's attitude and to

125

form a view of his experience and professionalism in this respect while evaluating his proposals.

Examine the Vendor's Commercial Approach
When you are satisfied that the field is narrowed to organisations capable of meeting your needs, examine the approach of the remaining contenders and check out the following attitudes.

(a) Is the vendor making realistic promises to get your job – can you keep him to these promises?
(b) Is his estimate and proposed solution based upon your needs?
(c) Has the vendor produced provisional schedules which demonstrate budgeted resource requirements.
(d) Are the schedules credible, and sufficiently detailed to be reviewed?

The commercial basis of the proposed contract is naturally based closely upon the schedule, the number of people the software agency has to provide and for how long. If the schedule is not based upon a reasonable analysis of the project, then the estimated price that the agency quotes is probably not valid. If you have secured a fixed-price contract for the whole job, then, provided the vendor is considered by you to be a secure organisation against whom you can take redress, it may be worth accepting the proposal. It is advisable, however, not to be triumphant about obtaining the cheapest quote in the shortest timescale unless you feel the vendor can meet your needs.

It is almost certain that a fixed-price quoted for a complete system before the detailed design is agreed will be based upon a contract which allows the vendor to increase charges in the event of you failing to meet agreed commitments or of changes in design principles. Make sure that you ask the vendor to specify these things in writing to you. It is better to know them at the beginning rather than to receive surprises later.

If the contract is agreed on a time and materials basis, in part or wholly, then understand the rate structure and the various grades and qualities of staff to be supplied. Know also the expense scales attached to travel and visits to your site and agree these. Negotiate also rates to be applied for overtime work. Ask for discounts for long-term staff-hire assignments.

If the basic rate structure is known, and a sufficiently detailed schedule has been produced, it is possible to estimate the price mark-up being used for the fixed-price parts of the contract. Comparison of different proposals will allow you to determine whether the difference in prices quoted is attributable to the basic schedule or the rate per man, or simply to the level of profit the vendor is seeking.

Even if you are able to negotiate a very competitive price for the fixed-price parts of the contract, it is advisable to arrange a separate staff-hire contract for the project manager. In this way, you can ensure his full-time commitment. His work commitment will not be something which you can forecast from the beginning, and it is important to have continuity in this function.

The Fee Contract

The ideal contract is one which penalises a party where the project estimate is exceeded owing to matters which they have not controlled; and which, at the same time, affords each party protection from mistakes or a lack of energy on the part of the other. Such contracts are difficult to arrange in the development of a systems application because many of the activities are interdependent.

The fee contract is a technique sometimes used to balance the responsibilities and risks involved in a project.

(a) The client has a degree of protection in that the profit taken from the project remains fixed, because any work provided over and beyond the original estimate is provided at cost price.
(b) The supplier is protected from heavy losses in the event of a major escalation of the project, although he does not take excess profit if this happens.

The basis of the contract is that there are two elements of the charge:

(a) A management fee paid in fixed instalments upon completion of agreed project milestones which represents the profit element in the contract.
(b) Charges based upon resources applied to the project and charged at cost rates previously agreed.

Of course, the setting of the cost rate and agreement upon what items it should include is a matter for negotiation between the two parties. This could be a protracted process, but it is certainly worthwhile when setting up such a commercial arrangement for a large project. The following suggestions are made:

Included in fee	Included in cost rate
Profit	Salary
Marketing costs	Social security
Provision for sickness	Pensions
Management costs	Accommodation
	Services
	On-site expenses

This type of contract allows the contractor to make excess profits only by completing the job well within the original estimates. This outcome should not cause the client any heart-searching, because his project will be producing benefits earlier and his total implementation cost will have been kept within initially agreed bounds.

Machine Time

Machine time for development work can be a large part of the costs of the project. It is important to establish how these costs are covered in the contract. If the costs are all to be included in the supplier's price, this becomes entirely a matter for him to consider, though he is probably not going to be willing to quote for amounts of time required in system trials and implementation when progress may be dependent upon the customer. This is also a part of the project where it is to be expected that the machine-time volumes will be high, and estimating most difficult.

If the purchaser has his own installation, it is usual for him to want to provide the machine time for the project since this minimises the external payments that he has to make and avoids him having to meet the profit and overhead costs of a third party. Where the customer does provide the machine time, there are two positions again to be safeguarded.

(a) The software agency will want to be sure that it can get access to machine time in the right amounts at the right time.
(b) The customer will require the software agency to forecast requirements and work within budgets which are agreed.

Procedures for dealing with this aspect of the contract can be established between the two parties as early in the project as possible. It is important to ensure that an adequate test cell is available to provide machine time to the project; delays and consequent costs can be excessive unless adequate arrangements are made.

Software Packages

The computer services industry has addressed itself repeatedly to the concept of the computer package, i.e. to the creation of a software product which has general application to a whole class of data-processing user. Examples might include a standard payroll package, an inventory management package or a production control package. Usually these packages have certain features which allow tolerance in the format of input and output and permit a degree of adaptation to the particular user's environment.

It is, perhaps, an overstatement to say that the main value of many packages has been in the marketing posture that they afford to the vending agency. An initial investment in systems and software design is made to pay off several times for the on-going cost of a support and maintenance team. We should not be critical of the concept, for it is a valuable contribution to lessening the software industry's tendency to re-invent the wheel. However, buyers have a right to be sceptical, and you should seek answers to the following questions:

128

(a) Does the package really meet your needs in functional terms?

(b) Is the package flexible enough to be tuned to the specific inputs and output formats required?

(c) How does the cost of the initial package and its further support and maintenance charges equate with the costs of a tailor-made system?

(d) What additional costs are incurred in tailoring the system to meet the specific needs of your company?

(e) What experience have previous users had using the package? Do you understand the benefits and limitations that they have encountered?

(f) What are the costs of running the package, and what will be the throughput on your machine?

(g) How do the running costs and throughput performance of the package compare with a tailor-made system?

(h) What are other people paying for the package? (Profits are often high after the vendor's original costs have been secured, and there is usually room to negotiate.)

(i) What kind of support and maintenance service is available?

Packages have been particularly valuable when applied to specific technical fields where the problem can be readily defined by logic. In the general commercial field of application, however, it is often difficult to design an efficient and comprehensive system which caters for the organisational quirks of several users and can interface with existing systems.

Performance Needs
When a contract is placed to purchase an application system, it is necessary to specify the performance required from the end product. This needs to be done at the beginning of the contract, and the significance of key performance criteria must be reflected in the contractual responsibilities placed upon the supplier.

From the purchaser's point of view, there are probably three major factors to consider:

(a) The amount of computer hardware that must be dedicated to the application when it is operational.

(b) The rate of throughput that the system must provide to cater for volumes of data in the time available.

(c) The speed and response which the system provides in processing transactions.

These criteria will need to be built into the design from the beginning, because it may be very expensive to change such performance criteria later. The criteria should be established with a view to considering any expansion in the business in future, and specific consideration should be given to the implications of increasing hardware resources, more remote terminals, volumes of transactions, file sizes and frequency of processing.

It is reasonable to expect the buyer to supply formally information to

129

the vendor which defines the performance required. Where such information is not supplied, or is given incorrectly, then it is unlikely that the vendor can be held accountable.

Project Dependencies

The progress of the project may, typically, be 70 per cent in the hands of the software agency and 30 per cent in the hands of the user. Both parties can cause unnecessary delay by failing to keep to their specified commitments.

It is expensive to the software agency to have delays in progress. The project team cannot be scheduled at short notice, and once a plan has been made, the project manager will expect to bring key people into and out of the project efficiently so as to stay within cost estimates. The sorts of thing which can delay progress include:

(a) Failure to deliver hardware on time.
(b) Substandard hardware performance.
(c) Shortage of planned machine time.
(d) Non-availability of user departments for training and induction to the system.
(e) Lateness in preparation of site to receive the hardware.
(f) Lateness of user-supplied test data, or lateness of basic data to create initial files for the system.
(g) Insufficient clerical effort to operate data control procedures.

SUMMARY OF CHAPTER 8

1 Subcontracting work to a software house is common throughout industry, and is particularly done by smaller companies who do not wish to support a large permanent data processing department.
2 Subcontracting projects is not simply a convenient way of passing off responsibility. There are many penalties to be incurred if the choice of subcontractor is bad, or if the correct working relationship is not established.
3 Terms of reference must be established so that a clear understanding is reached of the complexity and nature of the service to be provided.
4 A typical software contract can be broken down into project milestones which serve as reference points for the different project stages. The stages can be considered as either:
    (a) Stages in which activities are interdependent and require detailed collaboration between both parties suggesting a time and materials contract against budgetary cost estimates.
    (b) Stages which are the software agency's sole responsibility and suitable for treatment as fixed-price contracts.
5 The purchaser should always allow the software agency sufficient time to study the requirement at the beginning, so that project budgets are set as realistically as possible.

6 Quotations should be supported by detailed schedules for each stage, and the budgetary estimates should be justified by figures for man-effort, machine time and charging rates.

7 Competitive tendering is to be encouraged, but too many tenders often mean that insufficient attention is given to the needs of individual tenderers and the evaluation of their proposals.

8 The purchaser should:
  (a) Assess the quality of staff proposed.
  (b) Ensure the nominated staff are truly available.
  (c) Interview staff.
  (d) Ask for named people in key roles.
  (e) Ensure that the project manager has a background of success and is available for a full-time commitment.

9 Review the documentation standards, and project management control standards used by the software agency, and secure evidence of their application in previous situations.

10 Evaluate the commercial approach of the software houses; be satisfied that the one chosen has correctly evaluated the work content of the project and has priced his quotation accordingly.

11 Do not take the cheapest price, unless you are convinced that it is going to secure you a contract with a credible organisation which can meet its promises.

12 Beware of contract clauses which allow the vendor to escalate the price, but look for sensible milestones to review the project and the options to continue with the vendor.

13 Ensure that the organisation which gets your order is big enough to put right any dissatisfaction that you may develop.

14 Consider the fee contract which places limits upon the profit made by the agency in the event of a major escalation of the work.

15 Budget for machine time and other expenditure incurred by the agency, establish responsibility for the provision of machine time at various stages of the project, and determine the responsibility for meeting machine costs.

16 Evaluate carefully the relevance and costs of any software packages offered as part of a proposal. The flexibility of a package and the possibility of adapting it to meet your specific needs is a most important consideration.

17 Ensure that, as a purchaser, you have specified the performance needs of your system before detailed design begins, including:
  (a) The amount of computer hardware dedicated to the application.
  (b) The rate of system throughput.
  (c) The responsiveness of the system to users.

18 Finally, know what your commitments are to the project before it is under way. Remember that, in project development, wasted time costs money and late activities on the critical path can delay the work on many other activities.

Chapter 9

Systems Audit for Cost Monitoring

The Service Provided by Systems Audit

The audit function within an organisation may be an aggressive force designed to keep the management of a company on its toes by monitoring and reporting upon performance of individual departments, identifying weaknesses and compelling line managers to take corrective action. It may, however, have a less controversial role of simply monitoring the company's procedures to ensure that resources and assets are safe from deliberate fraud, or are not unintentionally put at risk.

Traditionally, these tasks are performed by a special department reporting to the financial controller and sometimes to the chief executive of the organisation. The degree of emphasis placed upon auditing functions depends, to a large extent, upon the size of the company, the complexity of the organisation, the degree to which responsibilities are decentralised and the general management style adopted within the organisation.

With the increasing use of computers, those aspects of auditing which are concerned with the efficiency and security offered by company procedures have taken on a new complexity. The traditional auditor will find many areas in information processing where his knowledge is severely taxed. Too often nowadays the company is placed more and more in the hands of computer people and the mystique that they generate. There is clearly a need for more specialised knowledge of EDP techniques within the auditing function.

Should the audit department use a thief to catch a thief, i.e. should they employ computer systems and programming specialists within the audit department? Or is it sufficient to rely upon traditional auditing staff who have been trained to have a certain familiarity with EDP techniques, and who possess a well-developed instinct to get to the bottom of things? Whatever the choice, there is one very significant problem: most people who have specialised in data processing work will want to develop their career with the EDP organisation!

Alternatively, should the systems audit function be something quite specific and separate from the traditional management audit? In a large company which has several operating divisions, each having their own data processing departments, this concept has some significance. The traditional internal audit department concerns itself with management problems and the security and legal aspects of company procedures and methods of accounting. On the other hand, the systems audit department concerns itself with supporting the internal audit department in examining the computer aspects and also investigating the various computer departments and commenting upon their efficiency and adherence to corporate EDP standards.

Thus we may consider the systems audit to have two distinct aims:

(a) To examine and report independently upon the effectiveness of controls in company systems.
(b) To examine and report upon the efficiency of data processing departments and computer installations.

In this chapter we will look at some of the ways in which these functions can be performed and suggest when and how the systems audit department should become involved in the development of systems.

In the following sections, we will introduce some of the key areas in which the systems audit team may operate. Before going through the details, however, we should stress that it is never too early for a systems auditor to get involved – it is far better that the auditor be consulted and given information from the very beginning of a new project rather than be brought in when it is too late to influence the detailed design. It is good practice to get the audit people to sign off acceptance of all systems documentation, including all assignment briefs and systems definitions produced by the systems department.

Organisational Aspects of Control
With the general tendency to create systems which span traditional department boundaries, the designers are faced with difficult political and communication problems. There is to the auditor, however, a clear advantage in that the possibility of deliberate fraud is much reduced by rendering it difficult to 'fix' the system except by collusion of many employees on a large scale. The ability to 'fix' a system is one of the key aspects to watch in any system, but particularly so in a computer system where programmers have the ability to build features into the computer procedures which make fraud difficult to detect.

Those who control the input and receive and distribute the output produced by computer systems are, similarly, in a position to arrange deliberate misuse of company resources. This category may include operators, the quality control staff in the computer department and the data control staff in the user departments. Provided the control procedures are arranged so that control and monitoring functions are shared between these people, one can feel confident that no single party can arrange to defraud the organisation without it being apparent to the others.

It is also important to check those controls which are designed to prevent inadvertent errors. The computer operations area is particularly vulnerable in this respect. The procedures-controlling media, containing input, output and up-to-date master files, are all important. The use of the wrong file at the wrong time in the cycle of operations for a system can produce very incorrect results and have a damaging effect, perhaps far outweighing the effects of a carefully planned and repetitive fraud. These aspects can be covered by examining the data processing department in two ways.

(a) By reviewing the systems designed by the data processing department for use throughout the company.
(b) By examining the internal operation of the data processing department and the procedures that it uses to carry out its function.

It is regretfully true that users may find it time-consuming to operate an elaborate control system, and may persuade the analysts to place less stringent demands upon the user's data control staff in order to gain more ready acceptance of the new procedures. This underlines the need for audit staff to monitor the design of the system and to authorise the design before it is released for program development and implementation.

The organisational weaknesses in control can certainly exist in both user departments and the data processing department itself, and the auditors should approach their investigations by looking diligently for concentration of duties which are not consistent with the concept of the separation of control responsibilities.

The first stage in the investigation will be to examine the organisation and the theoretical responsibilities of departments and individuals within departments. This must be compared with what happens in practice to ensure that the system under review provides for cross-checks upon transactions by different individuals in different units of the organisation. A clear example is the separation of the data control function from the data preparation function, with a proper system of control accounts to monitor the transfer of data.

There should, of course, be clear written specifications of the duties of all individuals within an organisation. In practice, we all know that this is idealistic. An organisation which claims to be dynamic will be very flexible in the way in which work gets done. To over-emphasise the need for detailed terms of reference for all individuals is anathema to some managements. However, when we are concerned with large volumes of information to be handled as discrete transactions, we do need to know who is responsible for the following operations:

(a) The initial gathering of source data.
(b) The conversion of this data to documents, or into machine input media.

134

(c) The collection and batching of transactions where this is necessary.
(d) The maintenance of control accounts to monitor the correct transmission of transactions through various stages of processing.
(e) The validation of data and the control over both valid transactions and the correction and acceptance of invalid transactions.

Similar considerations apply to the responsibilities for processing information in the computer operations unit, and for the distribution of output. A chain of responsibilities must be examined, including:

(a) Authorising a computer run or a change in computer schedules.
(b) Balancing control accounts generated in computer processing with those created in data collection.
(c) Reviewing the correct use of file media and the sequence of operations performed in the computer system.
(d) Performing quality control checks upon output.
(e) Checking for errors, correcting errors and monitoring that errors are at an acceptable level.
(f) The correct and efficient distribution of output.

Control of Data

Data is expensive to generate, and the costs of inaccurate data may be startlingly high. The establishment of controls to monitor the correct movement of data are of paramount importance for an information system. It follows that the verification of the adequacy of the design in providing such controls is a primary task of the systems auditor; as is the surveillance of the use of these controls in everyday operation of the live system.

The conditions to be checked in the movement of data include the loss of complete transactions, batches of transactions, the loss or corruption of certain fields within transactions, or the accumulation of unwanted data. The systems auditor should satisfy himself of the efficiency of the procedures and techniques used to achieve these safeguards, and identify the individuals responsible for carrying out such functions.

The task of the systems auditor is to protect the organisation from both deliberate fraud and the neglect of individuals who may destroy the value and credibility of the company's main systems. The techniques used are many and varied, according to the nature of the system under review. It is, however, true to say that the more one approaches communications-based systems using real-time techniques, the more essential it is for the auditor to be able to check out the strengths and weaknesses of the computer procedures internal to the computer itself. The responsibility of such systems are generally so much more significant than batch systems, since the concentration of functions within the computer tends to be more intense, and the reactions and effect upon the organisation more immediate.

135

Computer Procedure Controls

The detection of deliberate frauds in the computer procedures is a task for someone who has experience in the development of computer systems. However, not every company can afford a large audit department, and not every audit department can offer a worthwhile career to a computer specialist. In many companies, therefore, the auditors regard the computer system as a 'black box' which can be tested by operating the system within some controlled environment to monitor its performance under test conditions.

This type of test can, if it is well organised, identify the kinds of weakness which stem from poor system design. It is not likely to yield any great information about deliberate frauds built into the system. For the latter purpose, therefore, many organisations will be advised to retain an expert to carry out periodic surveys, or to consider hiring an appropriate consultant to do this work on their behalf.

The most difficult kind of fraud to detect is one which is built into the logic of a program, e.g. to direct cash to 'phantom' accounts, or to allow goods to be delivered to an apparent customer's address without raising the necessary invoicing documentation. Such procedures can be written into the programs so that they are only activated by some condition present in the data at run time. For example, the presence of a particular account code could activate such a routine. People who are determined enough to carry out such frauds are capable of supplying sufficient thought to the problem for the control accounts to be balanced throughout the operation of the system. Thus, such a fraud can remain undetected, even though the system is subject to the most rigorous tests with test data.

The kind of safeguards to be taken require a knowledge of programming and computer procedure design. The systems documentation and programming specifications have to be checked out in detail to ensure that they accurately reflect the system requirements. Every line of code in the programs has to be checked to see that it is pertinent and relevant to the specifications, and linkages throughout the system have to be traced to see that unauthorised routines are not activated.

When a program has been checked out in this level of detail, the auditor should take a copy of the program and keep it in a safe at a location not available to the computer personnel. Thus spot-checks can be made by comparing this version of the program with versions in use from time to time. All amendments to the program will have to be authorised by the auditors, who will need a secure procedure for updating their master copy.

This procedure is, of course, quite cumbersome and costly to retain, and it is a matter for managerial judgement as to whether this kind of monitoring is essential in particular cases.

System Flaws

To monitor the design of a computer system successfully to identify the flaws which will put the cash or resources of the company at risk requires the knowledge and experience of a systems designer. It is not possible in this chapter to identify all the factors which have to be considered, but some are described below.

One of the most important conditions to avoid in a system is the entry of unauthorised or invalid data. The systems designer has to study the requirements of the business in this respect and build controls into the system to identify and reject transactions which do not fulfil the requirements. The systems auditor, in verifying the design, or in examining the system subsequently in live situations, has to check that these controls are up to date and reflect the changing circumstances of the business. The following examples have to be considered :

(a) Data entering the system as transactions or inquiries must contain the authorisation of appropriate users.
(b) The validity checks must ensure that data entering the system is complete within each transaction and group of transactions.
(c) Control accounts must be operated to check that data is not lost or corrupted at intermediate stages of processing.
(d) Codes used – for example, account numbers or product identifications – must be checked for validity. Check digits or range checks, or checks for logical combinations of codes should be considered.
(e) Checks must be carried out by programmers at run time to ensure that the correct data files are addressed.
(f) Procedures for restarting computer runs after breakdowns must be such that they afford complete protection against file corruption or loss or duplication of transactions.
(g) The correct sequencing of transactions must be checked in some cases.
(h) Programming techniques should include logical checks upon the methods used to derive results in calculations.
(i) Checks against incorrect action by operators should be included to save machine time and materials which might otherwise be wasted in incorrect runs.

It will be appreciated that many of these areas require business knowledge, and some require technical knowledge of computing. It is possible for many of these auditing functions to be carried out by a financial audit department supported by relevant technical staff. The technical staff could be own staff, or hired temporarily from an outside agency specialising in computer security and system audit.

The situation in many small companies is such that they cannot retain a specialist on their own staff because they cannot offer such an individual career development. In many such companies, auditing never goes beyond the kind of procedural audit obtained from a traditional financial audit department.

Corporate Data Processing Audits
In large organisations where separate divisions run their own data pro-

137

cessing operations, it has become increasingly popular to establish an audit function to ensure:

(a) That resources are fully utilised and duplication is avoided.
(b) That specific standards are adopted in common throughout the group.

The audits are conducted to ensure that individual data processing units are maintaining good control over their operations and developments. The following headings should be considered as essential for this purpose:

Hardware: All equipment in use at each installation will be listed and valued. The objective is to ensure the compatibility of hardware throughout the group, that the throughput capacity of the installations are assessed regularly and that the throughput achieved is monitored.

Surplus equipment can also be identified for withdrawal or for transfer to another site in need of the hardware concerned. All future acquisitions have then to be vetted and approved by the data processing audit department to ensure that they are in line with the needs of local units; and that they form part of a co-ordinated distribution of hardware throughout the group.

Operations: Machine performance must be maintained to monitor the performance of individual machines and installations in terms of availability, serviceability and throughput.

The capacity of the installation should be examined in relation to the number of shifts worked and the optimum throughput. The balance of each installation should be assessed in terms of processor speed, core store, input and output devices and secondary store.

Systems development work: If we accept that it is important to evaluate the efficiency of the hardware utilisation at any particular installation, it follows that there is a need to monitor the value derived from individual applications. It is pointless having an efficient machine operation if the applications themselves are not contributing real benefits to the organisation. The central control of applications development, or the monitoring of the planned developments from the centre, represents a very firm policy which is bound to involve the systems audit function in very detailed interaction with the various units in a multidivisional organisation.

I refer back to Chapter 1 (page 17) for an analysis of the problems, and for a justification for this level of interaction between the centre and the different operating units which have separate data processing departments. There is little point in compromise here. If the systems audit function is asked to ensure that all data processing units are operating efficiently, it must set the standards and ground rules which are to be used to influence local data processing departments and to measure their success.

The following guidelines demonstrate one method of monitoring system development in the various data processing units, and are concerned initially with the justification and authorisation of new projects.

Priorities and Justification

All new projects should be approved by the local data processing unit, the local line management and the systems audit unit. Priorities should be assigned to projects according to whether the financial justification for the project is sound (refer back to Chapter 4), but also the following criteria can be considered.

Priority 1: A new system designed to help a department meet its objectives.

Priority 2: A new system with substantial financial benefits, but not essential to help any particular unit achieve its objectives.

Priority 3: A new system with intangible benefits, and not essential to helping a unit achieve its objectives.

All planned developments should be allowed to proceed only if the local data processing department, the local line management and the systems audit department agree.

Project Development

The systems audit should also give their attention to projects under development to ensure that systems are being created in accordance with the original objectives; and the project control methods should be examined to see whether the standards indicated previously in Chapter 3 (page 48) are being fulfilled. The attitude towards the project should be looked at critically to see whether a positive response is made to the problems encountered in development. The emphasis placed upon target setting and the significance of major milestones in planning and reviewing the progress and technical quality of the project are essential factors to examine.

Existing Production Systems

The existing production systems in each installation should be reviewed to see whether they are achieving the required level of performance and, more specifically, whether they are helping the users to achieve their own objectives. The security and control aspects of each system will also be examined, as suggested earlier in this chapter.

The existing systems should be examined to ascertain their resilience and robustness to the changing environment in which they have to operate, and the reasons for system failures should be diagnosed. If the system has to undergo frequent amendments, the level of maintained activity and the reasons and costs incurred should be reported.

An audit of this nature may point to the need to redevelop existing systems and provide an opportunity for a critical review of an important area of the organisation's business.

General Efficiency Audit

The data processing unit can also be examined for internal efficiency. There are many big-expenditure areas within data processing, and also areas of great risk for the organisation. The following activities should be included in a data processing audit:

(a) Internal procedures and work flow.
(b) Security:
      (i) Physical security of equipment and media.
      (ii) Security of information.
(c) Reproduction methods and costs.
(d) Use of consumable materials, stationery cards, ribbons, paper tape, etc.
(e) Standards of job control and organisation of work before computer operation.
(f) Operating standards and procedures.
(g) Programming standards and procedures.
(h) Systems standards and procedures.
(i) Staff establishments and actual staff numbers and grades.
(j) Current and capital expenditure against budgets.
(k) Chargeout methods and costing techniques.
(l) Organisation structure.
(m) Fire hazards and precautions.

The Organisational Position of Systems Audit

At the beginning of the chapter, we noted that there is a conflict concerning the financial aspects of auditing and the computing aspects of the work of systems audit staff. The issue is not easily resolved but one becomes increasingly aware of the need for computing and data processing knowledge in internal audit work. Furthermore, the dispersal of expensive computer installations in large multidivisional organisations establishes the need for an audit of the data processing function in its own right. Figure 9.1 suggests a compromise, in which the chief of the internal audit department and the corporate data processing manager (to whom the systems audit department reports) operate as part of the same management team. The two kinds of audit department must obviously collaborate to make the best use of their specialists' skills, but if they can be made to work in this way, they can open up backward areas of the organisation: first, by exposing weaknesses which are lowering the efficiency of the company, and then by providing the technical skills to indicate solutions and implement improved systems in collaboration with the data processing units in line divisions.

    Used in this way, the systems audit function can be a powerful force to stimulate organisational efficiency.

Figure 9.1   *The organisational position of the systems audit department.*

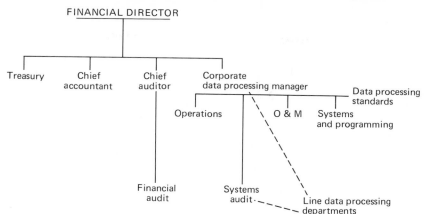

SUMMARY OF CHAPTER 9

1   The systems audit function has become more specialised with the advent of computers, giving rise to the suggestion that traditional internal audit departments are not able to cope with monitoring the efficiency and security of their organisation's procedures.

2   A computer specialist will usually wish to develop his career in data processing rather than in financial auditing, and for this reason traditional audit departments find it difficult to recruit and retain people able to audit computer procedures.

3   There is a case in large organisations for having an internal audit department within the central finance group, and a systems audit department as part of the central management services group.

4   A systems audit department should be given two primary objectives:
  (a)   To examine and report independently upon the effectiveness of controls in systems operated throughout the organisation.
  (b)   To examine and report upon the efficiency of data processing departments and computer installations within the organisation.

The first of these objectives should be fulfilled by operating with and in support of the internal audit department.

5   All new system developments should be authorised by the systems audit department after the initial design is completed and before money is expended in detailed implementation.

6   The systems audit department should review systems to ensure that controls are effective and to ensure that the possibility of deliberate fraud is minimised by the separation of control responsibilities.

7   Responsibilities for control mechanisms must be formally established

to cover all activities from the initial gathering of source data through to the distribution of output.

8　The systems auditor must use his skill to protect an organisation both from deliberate fraud and from the neglect of individuals.

9　The detection of deliberate fraud is most difficult where the mechanisms to perpetrate the fraud have been carefully built into the computer procedures. A specialist in computer procedures is needed to identify and trace these conditions.

10　Systems audit should retain copies of all programs, and monitor amendments made. Spot-checks must then be made to ensure that only the authorised versions of programs are being used in live production work.

11　The systems audit department should also be given responsibility to audit the various data processing units throughout a group to ensure:

(a) That resources are fully utilised and duplication is avoided.

(b) That common standards are adopted throughout the group.

12　The authority of systems audit should be extended to include:

(a) Hardware compatibility.

(b) Financial approval of hardware expenditure.

(c) Monitoring efficiency of installations.

(d) Monitoring of system developments.

(e) Efficiency audit of existing systems.

(f) Monitoring the use of data processing management standards.

(g) Physical security of installations and data.

13　The systems audit and internal audit can, when working in collaboration with one another, cover the complete range of an organisation's auditing needs. In large divisional companies, where communications are difficult, they can identify weakness and problems, and suggest solutions. In this way, inefficient areas of the company can be opened up for improvement, and, where necessary, the corporate data processing authority can bring its resources to bear to implement the solutions. Thus the systems audit department becomes a powerful tool for formulating and sustaining corporate data processing policy and standards.

Chapter 10

Cost Efficiency in Data Processing Operations

Opportunities for Cost Control

The costs of the computer operations department is, typically, about 60 to 70 per cent of the total expenditure budget for a medium-sized data processing unit. The primary items included in the operations budget are:

(a) Costs of floor space.
(b) Machine rental or capital depreciation.
(c) Personnel.
(d) Media (stationery, magnetic media).
(e) Maintenance charges.

It is perhaps odd that a department with such a large expenditure budget should be left to grow without any real check upon its efficiency or the relevance of many of the tasks that it performs. Unfortunately, this is often the case. The computer operations department merely handles work generated by others, and is itself very seldom consulted about the requirements of the job that it performs for other people. Every day brings a fresh volume of work consisting of either routine production work from user departments, or ad hoc procedures and program development work from the systems department.

It is in the operations area that many companies waste opportunities to make their whole computing plan cost-effective. Consider, first, two of the main areas in which we can create control over operational costs:

(a) The physical space occupied by a computer and its ancillary media and equipment usually requires to be air-conditioned and environmentally controlled. By minimising the amount of hardware required in the computer configuration, it is possible to contain the size of the physical space and the environmental conditioning. The cost of floor space alone is not insignificant, particularly in city areas.
(b) Minimising the amount of equipment also directly reduces rental and

maintenance costs for the total configuration; and the direct labour costs associated with the operating and support staff.

The number-one aim therefore is to minimise the size of the hardware configuration consistent with providing an adequate resource to run the production work and to develop any new systems required. Methods of work measurement in the computer operations department are necessary to measure and monitor the efficiency with which the department operates the hardware, and to ascertain the spare capacity available for further work. In short, it is necessary to see that work is being put through the machine efficiently and economically and that there are benefits associated with the production of that work.

The computer operations department can be considered as the key point of a production process, into which raw material (data) is fed, and from which finished products (information) are obtained. The process can be speeded up by being more efficient as well as by applying additional production resources. Improved efficiency should be a continuing aim; but application of additional resources will only be justified if the benefits introduced significantly exceed the additional cost. Benefits which can arise from increased efficiency include:

(a) Reduction in man-effort required (e.g. shift reduction).
(b) Reduction in hardware rental and maintenance charges.
(c) Reduction in magnetic media and stationery requirements.
(d) Reduction in physical space.
(e) Control over capital invested in environmental conditioning.
(f) Creation of capacity for new projects.
(g) Improvements in the efficiency of user departments.
(h) Faster development of projects.

It is necessary to look frequently at the value of the work being done to decide whether or not some production jobs should be redesigned or abandoned altogether, thus creating more capacity for more beneficial developments. This topic has been dealt with more fully in Chapter 9, which deals with system audits.

There are many factors outside the immediate control of the computer operations department which will affect the efficiency with which this department can operate. For example, programs which have been written in an inefficient manner may occupy an unwarranted amount of time and storage resources when operational. We have to look outside the computer operations department to the systems and programming department for a solution in these cases.

It is also necessary to consider quality of output: is it accurate, timely and in accordance with the standards agreed with the user as part of the system design? If results are not of a suitable quality, it needs to be

144

ascertained whether this is again inherent in the design of the system, or whether it can be attributed to bad operating standards.

To summarise, any review of the computer operations facility and its budget should first commence with an examination of individual systems to ascertain:

(a) Is the work being run efficiently, and if not, are the causes:
    (i) Within the immediate control of the computer department's operational staff?
    (ii) Constrained by the original design of the system?
    (iii) Related to the hardware/software resources available?
    (iv) Affected by user departments' behaviour?
(b) Is the work being produced giving real benefits to the users, and if not, should the systems be:
    (i) Scrapped entirely?
    (ii) Redesigned to be of more benefit to users?
(c) Are the results that are being produced up to the standards of quality required by users, and if not, is this attributable to:
    (i) Poor operational control?
    (ii) Poor design standards in the first place?
    (iii) Poor data control by users?

Let us next look in more detail at the factors which have a bearing on the efficiency of the computer operations department, isolating those factors which are within the control of the operations staff and those which are outside their immediate responsibility.

Hardware Characteristics and Throughput

A given hardware configuration has certain physical constraints which place limits upon the amount of work which can be run in a given amount of time. These physical constraints, combined with characteristics of the application, should be balanced by the systems designer to achieve the most efficient computer procedure for the application concerned.

How can we measure the efficiency of a system, and be able to compare its performance with another? In practice this is very difficult, for no two applications do precisely the same job. The only clear measure of work performed in a given period has to be based upon such criteria as:

(a) The number of transactions handled.
(b) The number of records maintained.
(c) The number of reports produced.
(d) The number of printed lines produced.

We might take the view that the output is the only physical evidence of the productive utility of the system, and from this conclude that a system which produces more output in a given period is more efficient than one

145

which produces less output. It is not very helpful, however, to compare the number of payslips produced in a given amount of time by a payroll system with the number of statements produced in a sales ledger system. It is meaningful to make comparisons only if the systems concerned perform similar functions. A payroll may be compared with another payroll, but only if the functions covered by each are the same. One payroll may deal only with weekly salaried staff, another with hourly rated staff as well.

The only way to evaluate the efficiency of an operations department is to establish some theoretical norm for the throughput of any given application, based upon the hardware configuration and the volume of records, inputs and outputs handled. Schedules are then established for running the application, and records are kept to effect comparisons of the time taken to run the application on successive occasions. In practice, there will be various aspects of the operation which can be altered to effect an improvement in the throughput of the system, and to approach, or improve upon, the theoretical figure.

Figure 10.1   *Schematic of a hardware configuration.*

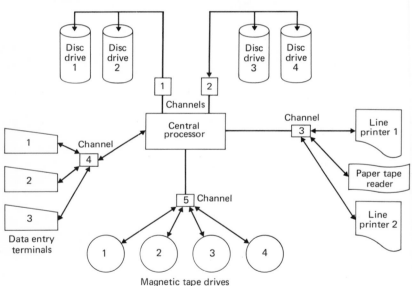

Figure 10.1 shows a typical hardware configuration. The peripheral units are all connected to the processor by channels, and in this case two channels are available to service two independent groups of disc drives. Because a channel can only handle one input/output transaction at a time, it follows that two disc units which are accessed simultaneously by the program will

146

work at less than maximum rate if they have to share the same input/output channel. Thus, the physical disposition of the disc files at run time will significantly affect throughput, and the operator must take note of this at run time. The configuration can be made less restrictive by acquiring additional channels.

A system can be tuned operationally by allocating resources to it in a certain manner. It can also, of course, be tuned by the programming and systems design people, who must balance activities within the application suite so that all peripherals used by the system are driven at continuous speeds close to the maximum possible for each device. When these two activities have been explored in depth, it remains to ensure that good operating procedures are adopted to keep the computer operating at full speed, and not allow the schedule to be delayed by failure to prepare for various activities which have to take place during the computer run, e.g the loading of files, input media, stationery, etc.

If all these factors are taken care of, an efficient computer operation will result. Near optimum performance may be achieved, and further substantial improvements will only then be possible by enhancing the hardware to improve the productive capability of the configuration. For example, faster tape decks may be procured, or a faster line printer, or more interface channels to handle input/output from the processor.

Multiprogramming: a Measure of Efficiency
Now this approach is all right as long as each system is regarded in isolation. The individual applications should be capable of being run in a time which approaches the theoretical maximum, given the requirements of the application and the hardware available. However, most general-purpose computers today are capable of controlling and operating several programs at the same time: the larger the configuration, and the more varied the array of peripherals available, the greater is the multiprogramming capability.

This tends to complicate life for the operations staff, because their scheduling task has many more parameters to consider. Assuming that the applications which they are running have been efficiently designed, they will interpret their objective as being to load the machine with work in such a manner that the various units of the computer are kept working at a very high rate – the idea being that the flow of output from the computer operations department will be increased as the various hardware units approach a higher degree of productive utilisation.

With multiprogramming, a configuration is necessary which has sufficient storage capacity and an array of peripherals to support the simultaneous operation of several programs. The computer applications must also be designed so that individual programs do not demand so many resources as to prevent there being enough equipment available to run another program at the same time.

Program suites have to be developed in accordance with constraints

147

placed upon the system designers to ensure that a high multiprogramming factor is achieved. The multiprogramming capability is usually estimated by considering the computer as being able to control a number of separate streams of production. Thus, if a computer configuration is able to support three streams of work, we would expect it to handle three independent jobs simultaneously. In practice, it will sometimes be running five or six jobs, and, on other occasions, two, or maybe only one.

Thus if, in a period of 10 elapsed hours, the operations department manages to process work equivalent to 25 hours on a single programming basis, then a multiprogramming factor of 2·5 has been achieved. A theoretical multiprogramming factor can thus be established for any particular configuration; and assuming that the applications conform to the design standards laid down to promote multiprogramming, this factor can be achieved over a long productive period.

The aim, when multiprogramming, is to utilise the computer more efficiently by enabling the central processor to be active more intensively than it would otherwise be when programs are run singly. The extreme difference between the speed of the internal memory operation and speeds of computer peripherals results in the processor being used in intermittent bursts when programs are run singly. For much of the time, the processor will be idle awaiting the transfer of data to or from peripheral units. However, in multiprogramming mode, the processor is able to activate other programs during these idle periods and to initiate other peripheral activities relating to those programs. If the right balance is achieved in loading a multiprogramming system, it can appear that several programs are being run at the same time, and peripherals will all appear to be operating at once.

In fact, individual programs will require a longer period of elapsed time within the machine, but a given volume of work relating to a group of independent jobs will be completed in less time than if the programs were run singly. A greater efficiency results, because a much higher degree of hardware utilisation is achieved.

The Importance of Operating Systems

The multiprogramming factor thus becomes a measure of the productivity of the computer operations department, and the operational staff should be aiming to improve this factor in everything that they do, whether it be producing today's running schedule, or planning next year's hardware enhancements.

With medium-sized and large-sized computers, the task of scheduling and controlling the hardware on a minute-by-minute basis becomes very difficult; the situation is so dynamic while the permutations of possible actions are too complex to guarantee optimum management of resources within the installation. It is to meet this situation that operating systems have been developed. Their purpose is to automate many of the procedures which operators would otherwise have to initiate manually. Thus, operating systems ease the problem of communication between the operator and the computer and take responsibility for routine actions.

Not the least significant of the benefits obtained from an operating system is the great reduction in the number of messages which have to pass between the operators' console and the supervisory program which co-ordinates activity within the configuration. The process of typing in commands, and printing out console messages for the operator, is without doubt very wasteful and causes significant delays where several programs are running simultaneously. The use of an operating system to pre-program the majority of the activities required greatly minimises such 'lost' time.

In practice, an operating system supervises the activities of several programs simultaneously, controlling the input and output to the various programs and passing control from one program to the next. The operating system is driven by job descriptions which are prepared as control instructions to describe the more routine activities which must take place, leaving the operators to intervene only when something unusual occurs or when physical effort is needed to load and unload files and input data.

There are usually several versions of a particular operating system, and these versions are designed to cater for different sizes and types of hardware configuration. It is very important to use the appropriate operating systems, as the following example illustrates.

The ICL 1900 range of computers is a completely modular hardware system with processors ranging from 16K words of storage to 256K words and upwards. A complete range of input/output and backing storage units is also available. Two main operating systems are available, apart from the manual executive which provides for operational control over the smaller processors.

The George 2 operating system provides a set of basic facilities which are ideal for machines up to 96K words of core, and George 3 is a full operating system with automatic scheduling facilities. There are many different versions of these two operating systems, but, for simplification, we cannot go into details here. In practice, the following guidelines apply:

Processors up to 16K words: Manual executive.
Processors from 32K to 96K words: George 2.
Processors from 96K words upwards: George 3.

However, because George 3 provides for more comprehensive facilities than George 2, it is often used by installations who desire the facilities but who do not have a configuration able fully to support them. As work builds up in such an installation, the productivity may drop alarmingly, and the only way out of this problem may be to revert to George 2 or to buy additional hardware. Operating systems like George 3 requires a lot of expertise to set up and maintain, but without such a system a large configuration can never be efficiently managed.

149

The choice of operating system is crucial to efficient computer utilisation, and it is worth acquiring special consultancy and guidance in making initial decisions and in setting up a task force to implement the initial applications.

Scheduling the Workload
Computer time is a very expensive resource, and the cost of a slack approach to computer scheduling and operation will be very considerable. The problem of scheduling is complex, and usually requires a specialised capability to be found only in a highly experienced individual. It is for this reason that, in successful departments, scheduling is done by a specific person or persons. The most common fault found in inefficient data processing departments is that no one really accepts responsibility for scheduling on a daily basis, and operators are allowed to progress work as they wish within the general framework of a weekly or monthly schedule. Apart from certain key jobs which have heavily underlined deadlines for delivery of output to user departments, the rest of the work may just be filled in as and when the operators think best.

Without some theoretical assessment of the best way to run a given shift of work, it is impossible to evaluate how well a team of operators are doing in practice. They may be achieving an unsatisfactory volume of throughput without anybody really knowing. If this goes on, it will eventually result in unnecessary capital expenditure to create a more powerful configuration as the workload expands.

In multiprogramming systems, the scheduling problem is, as we have seen, a very critical activity. Each application will require certain volumes and types of hardware resource, including core store, magnetic tape readers, disc drives, printers' card or paper tape readers. These requirements have to be mapped to suit the pattern of availability within the configuration while bearing in mind the time taken to execute various elements of each application. It is a difficult task, and not one to be attempted halfheartedly while trying to discharge some other demanding responsibility.

A particular day's schedule will, typically, be built around routine production work for which scheduled times for delivery of output have been agreed. The ad hoc work and the program and system development work has to be scheduled around this basic pattern. In the case of program development work, the operations department must usually guarantee a turnround of a given number of jobs in a given period of time. A programmer will expect at least one turnround per day.

Scheduling will enable an assessment to be made of the practicality of meeting the user's expectations for output, and will also establish the theoretical spare capacity within the installation in a given period of time.

This schedule has to be constantly compared with the practical achievements to see whether action can be taken to improve. If the schedule is realistic, and the standard of operating is good, one would expect to see that, over a given month, more than 90 per cent of the work is completed to time and that users are satisfied with both quality and timing. The records maintained to monitor the results being achieved by the operations department should entail a log of the time taken to run specific applications, plus more specific criteria related to each application which will provide a more definitive means of measurement, e.g. the number of transactions handled, the number of documents printed, the number of reports provided. Formal reports should be produced each week containing this information, along with explanations of variances in throughput.

Failure to achieve an expected level of performance must require a close examination to see where the problem lies. The various reasons which can emerge will fall under one of the following:

(a) Directly attributable to poor operating standards within computer operations.
(b) Affected by poor application design.
(c) Affected by the efficiency of hardware/software performance.
(d) Affected by user departments.

Efficiency and Operating Standards
The expenditure for purchasing, renting and maintaining computer hardware can be one of the most significant investment decisions made by an

Figure 10.2 *Work flow in a computer installation.*

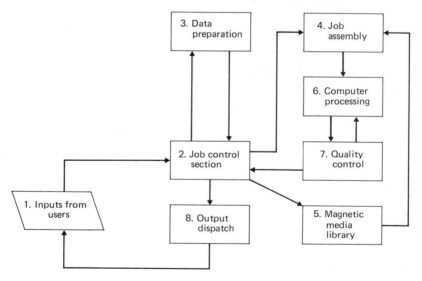

organisation. Having taken the decision, it is important not to squander the benefits by failing to establish an efficient operating environment.

151

The first factor to be considered is the physical layout of the installation, which must permit a constant flow of work to the computer and enable results to be distributed efficiently. The library of media must also be well organised to permit the flow of magnetic media files to and from the computer and to ensure that they are properly organised and protected at all times. Figure 10.2 shows the work flow within an installation.

The various hardware units must also be situated to permit operators to move about the installation in an efficient manner, without mutual interference. There should be adequate storage capacity outside the operating area to make certain that stationery and media, finished output and jobs waiting to be run are not hampering the efficiency of operations.

The operations staff should be thoroughly trained and experienced, and, above all, there must be enough staff to ensure that the configuration is adequately manned. If possible, each shift should be supported by reserve staff, or, in times of sickness and leave, cover should be found by employing temporary staff of the right quality from an outside agency. In practice I have observed that undermanning is one of the biggest single causes of poor throughput performance – particularly on large machines. The operations area is a place where heavy cost penalties are incurred by a shortage of staff, or by a failure to maintain people of the appropriate quality.

Many of the computers in use today are adequately manned only in the prime daytime shifts. Many machines are not manned at night or at weekends. This may result in savings in labour costs, but invariably leads to the acquisition of an expensive configuration that has more power than the organisation really needs while the actual productivity achieved is well below that which can be expected.

The efficient operation of the computer room is dependent upon the skill and discipline of the computer operations staff and upon the way in which they are organised. The objective is to ensure that the machine is not idle and that the various units forming the configuration are kept operating at something approaching their maximum rate. This, as we have seen, is achieved by scheduling the work well and by obtaining an appropriate mix of jobs. It is also achieved in many small ways by the manner in which work is executed by the operating team.

Every attempt must be made to anticipate the resources required by programs, and to make sure that they are available, e.g. stationery for the line printer, the allocation to programs of core store, the provision of appropriate files and so on.

Of course, it is not sufficient just to process the work speedily; the accuracy and quality of the output is all-important. A computer department which provides poor-quality results is a liability which cannot be tolerated. Procedures must be established to enable quality checks to be made continually during the running of an application so as to avoid the situation where several hours of computer time are consumed only to find that the results produced are unsatisfactory. If an application is designed which does not provide opportunities for diagnosing such situations, then the operations department would be justified in refusing to accept responsibility for the job as a routine operational task.

When a job is handed over by systems staff to the computer operations unit as a routine operational application, documentation should be provided, including operating instructions and job control procedures. These documents would have to be approved by the computer operations department, and a reasonable trial period should be allowed for them to satisfy themselves that the application and its documentation are of an acceptable standard. It is normal for the systems staff and programmers who have developed the application to provide support during this trial period, and particularly to assist in recovery if anything goes wrong. Before the application is finally handed over, the operations department must have successfully demonstrated their ability to stand on their own feet.

The efficiency of a particular team of operators is difficult to measure in absolute terms. In principle, this has to be established by the circumstantial evidence obtained by measuring the success they have in completing the work assigned to them. A manual log should be kept by the shift leader to record details of any stoppages and breakdowns occurring in the shift, and the reasons for these delays must be given. Action has to be taken to avoid a repetition of the stoppage, including any caused by factors outside the immediate control of the operations staff.

Most computers will produce a record of operator activities as a log printed on the console typewriter. An analysis of this log, in which every message passing between the console operator and the supervisory program is recorded chronologically, will reveal mistakes and delays caused by lack of training or inattention on the part of the operating team.

Measuring Productivity and Performance in Operations
So far, in this chapter, I have tried to demonstrate the complexity of establishing precise standards for performance measurement in the computer operations area. There are many interacting phenomena which may affect the throughput of work, and many of these cannot be controlled by the operations unit.

However, there must be some schedule established for the operation of the machine, and there must be a reporting system which identifies achievement against this schedule and also identifies the spare capacity available on the computer as a whole, and the degree of utilisation of individual units.

The reporting system must also compel the operations staff to indicate delays and time wasted in recovering from failures, and the reasons for delays and failures must be given. Over a period of time, therefore, a clear picture can be built up of the efficiency of the total operation, and the most consistent factors which affect performance can be diagnosed. This diagnosis will permit an assessment of the following:

153

(a) Efficiency of the operations teams.
(b) Effectiveness of media management.
(c) Quality of the hardware and maintenance provided.
(d) Reliability of software.
(e) Quality of the environment.
(f) Efficiency of individual suites and programs.
(g) Effect of application design upon multiprogramming.
(h) Quality of organisation and work flow to support applications.
(i) The level of support given by users.

Such a reporting system will isolate individual problems and enable corrective action to take place. The data processing management will also need to take an overall view of productivity. There are three possible ways of trying to measure the efficiency of computer operations, none of which will provide a completely satisfying and conclusive measure of performance. However, by taking all three together we can further isolate disturbing factors and measure the costs associated with specific actions to improve the efficiency of the total operation.

(a) In the first place, we can look at the performance of any individual application, establish theoretical running times for running it as a routine job for given volumes of transactions and measure achievements in practice. Where performance is consistently unsatisfactory, an evaluation of the development work required to improve the performance can be made, and a cost can thereby be placed upon improving efficiency of the application.
(b) Secondly, we can look at the operation as a whole and, over a period spanning several weeks or months, measure the useful output produced for a given set of applications and divide it by the number of hours allocated to produce that output in the period concerned. The number of hours allocated would have to include all time spent in rerunning spoilt work, but would not include time wasted owing to causes beyond the control of the operations unit, e.g. hardware failure.
(c) Thirdly, we can measure the useful output produced by the installation as a whole over a period of several weeks or months, and divide this by the number of hours that the machine is switched on to produce the given output.

The first of these methods is not too difficult to set up, and provides a valuable control for data processing management in monitoring the efficiency of the applications. The second and third methods suffer from the difficulty in being precise about what an output is, and the validity of comparing one type of output with another, e.g. comparing a list of debtors with a compilation listing. Assuming that one is prepared to grapple with such definitions, it is reasonable to accept that, if useful output is measured over a long period of time entailing a large number of outputs, comparisons of the results will enable valid assumptions to be made about overall efficiency.

The second method is intended specifically to monitor the effectiveness of the operations department in given periods of time, and it is best to avoid the inclusion of non-routine factors by restricting the analysis to a given set of applications which form the major routine production work-load for the installation.

The third method is aimed at measuring the overall effectiveness of the data processing department over a period of several weeks.

These calculations will, of course, produce ratios which have been achieved by fairly crude methods. Such methods should not be discarded for all that. They are particularly valuable for measuring the impact of additional production resources upon the installation in a given period, or for assessing the benefit obtained from the investment in a new operating system. For example, see Figure 10.3, which uses the third method above to evaluate the effect of introducing a different operating system for the first three months of a year. The ratio generated is the 'the number of useful outputs produced per hour of scheduled machine time'.

Figure 10.3   *The third method for evaluating an operating system.*

	Number of productive jobs	Number of useful reports	Number of Hours	Ratio
First month	200	1200	480	2·5
Second month	250	2000	550	3·36
Third month	260	2040	510	4

SUMMARY OF CHAPTER 10

1   The computer operations department is responsible for a major part of the expenditure (say 65 per cent) in a data processing department. It is an area in which there are usually many opportunities to curtail waste and improve efficiency.

2   The computer hardware, and the space that it occupies, along with its associated storage facilities for media and stationery, are major items of expense.

3   The prime need is to obtain a computer configuration which is power-ful enough to support the systems needed by the organisation, but which does not have superfluous capacity. Continual monitoring and review of hardware requirements is necessary to balance the growing needs for com-puter power and to ensure that outdated and inefficient systems are not allowed to survive.

4   It is necessary continually to review the quality and accuracy of all output to ensure that operational systems fulfil the needs for which they were originally designed.

5   There are four major causes of bad operational systems:

(a)   A system may be weak in its original design, and the systems

155

development department must be responsible for identifying and correcting these failings.

(b) The computer operations department may cause weakness by failure to observe good standards of operating and control.

(c) The users of a system may fail to support the system through ineffective control of data and failure to adhere to agreed procedures.

(d) The hardware may be poorly maintained or be overloaded by the total volume of work placed upon the installation.

6   Standards of measurement must be established for an installation to identify the throughput achieved for individual systems and for the workload as a whole.

7   Standards must be established for controlling the development of applications so that new computer systems are designed in accordance with rules established to obtain a balanced workload in the installation.

8   The operating system used in an installation must be chosen to obtain a balanced use of the hardware and must be implemented efficiently. Poor operating systems are a major cause of wasted machine capacity.

9   A computer installation must have detailed daily schedules which are maintained by a member of the operations team who is responsible to ensure that the hardware is efficiently loaded and utilised.

10   An installation in which daily scheduling is treated light-heartedly will inevitably contain excess amounts of equipment. One objective of scheduling is to review constantly the spare capacity of the configuration.

11   In a good installation, more than 90 per cent of the work will be regularly produced on time.

12   The physical layout of the installation is important. Do not expect efficient performance if the operators are not able to move about the installation efficiently without mutual interference.

13   Undermanning is a common and serious cause of low operating efficiency in computer operations.

14   Many computer installations are not staffed fully for more than two shifts per day. This invariably means that the installation acquires a much more powerful hardware configuration than is strictly necessary.

15   Operators must be fully trained, and the supervision needs to be first class to ensure that unnecessary idle time is not incurred.

16   The procedure to transfer responsibility for a new system from the systems department to the operations department must be formal, and it must allow for an extended period of support by the systems department until the operations department finally accepts responsibility.

17   A regular reporting system should be established to review achievements in running production work against previously agreed schedules.

18   The reporting system should compel the operations department to justify delays and time wasted in recovering from failures.

19   Persistent failures should be investigated and the objective of the operations manager must be continually to assess:

(a) Efficiency of operations team.
(b) Effectiveness and security of media management.
(c) Quality of the hardware.
(d) Effectiveness of the hardware maintenance.
(e) Reliability of software.
(f) Quality of the environment.
(g) Efficiency of individual program suites.
(h) Multiprogramming throughput efficiency.
(j) Effectiveness of work flow and quality control.
(k) The quality of support given by user departments.

Index